NATHAN ROTENSTREICH

ON FAITH

EDITED AND WITH A FOREWORD BY

Paul Mendes-Flohr

THE UNIVERSITY OF CHICAGO PRESS / CHICAGO AND LONDON

Nathan Rotenstreich (1914–1993) taught at the Hebrew University of Jerusalem and was visiting professor at the City University of New York, the University of Chicago, and Harvard University. (For further details, see foreword.) Paul Mendes-Flohr is professsor of philosophy at the Hebrew University of Jersalem.

The University of Chicago Press, Chicago 60637
The University of Chicago Press, Ltd., London
© 1998 by The University of Chicago
All rights reserved. Published 1998
Printed in the United States of America
06 05   04   03 02 01 00 99 98 1 2 3 4 5

ISBN: 0-226-72875-7 (cloth)
ISBN: 0-226-72876-5 (paper)

Library of Congress Cataloging-in-Publication Data

Rotenstreich, Nathan, 1914–93
    On faith / Nathan Rotenstreich ; edited with a foreword by
Paul Mendes-Flohr.
        p.   cm.
    Includes bibliographical references.
        ISBN 0-226-72875-7 (alk. paper). — ISBN 0-226-72876-5 (pbk. :
alk. paper).
        1. Faith.   I. Mendes-Flohr, Paul R.   II.   Title.
    BV4637.R68   1998
    218—dc21
                                                        97-40092
                                                        CIP

⊗ The paper used in this publication meets the minimum requirements of the American National Standard for Information Sciences—Permanence of Paper for Printed Library Materials, ANSI Z39.48-1984.

ON FAITH

CONTENTS

FOREWORD

This volume is published posthumously. Its author, Nathan Rotenstreich, died in 1993 at the age of seventy-nine. He was among the most eminent scholars in the State of Israel. At his death he was professor emeritus of philosophy at the Hebrew University of Jerusalem and vice-president of the Israel Academy of the Sciences and Humanities, of which he was a founding member. Born in 1914 in Sambor—then in the Austrian province of Galicia and now in Poland—Rotenstreich emigrated to Palestine in 1932. He earned his Ph.D. at the Hebrew University in 1938 with a dissertation entitled "The Problem of Substance in Philosophy from Kant to Hegel," and joined the faculty of his alma mater in 1951. Here he enjoyed a stellar career, eventually serving as the university's dean of humanities and rector. Awarded in 1963 the prestigious Israel Prize for the Humanities, Rotenstreich was acclaimed for his translations of Kant's works into Hebrew (initially undertaken together with his former teacher Shmuel Hugo Bergman). An awesomely prolific scholar, Rotenstreich published more than thirty books—most recently *Reason and Its Manifestations: A Study of Kant and Hegel,* also published posthumously[1]—and some six hundred scholarly articles (in English, French, German, and Hebrew). These writings are distinguished by a sustained interest in the history of philosophy,

1. Stuttgart-Bad Connstaat: Frommann-Holzboog, 1996. Spekulation und Erfahrung: Texte und Untersuchungen zum deutschen Idealismus, vol. 34.

both general and Jewish, and an elaboration of an original systemic philosophy.[2]

Widely acknowledged as a leading scholar of Kant and Hegel, Rotenstreich as a thinker can be best placed between—and beyond—both of them. In one respect specifically he regarded himself a Kantian. He followed the sage of Königsberg in assigning to reason an a priori transcendental role in the process of acquiring knowledge of the world. On the other hand, he did not accept Kant's radical dualism between the empirical and the transcendental; rather, he deemed the nexus between the transcendental subject and the object of knowledge to be dynamic and dialectical. He called himself, somewhat whimsically, a "mini-Kantian," or a "post-neo-Kantian." Like the neo-Kantians, however, he sought to extend philosophical analysis to embrace historical and cultural aspects of human civilization,[3] as is exemplified by the theme of the present volume. From Hegel and his disciples, Rotenstreich inherited an appreciation of history as the dynamic context of thought, although he decidedly rejected the Hegelian assumption that history is endowed with an immanent rationality.

This book emerges from Rotenstreich's critical engagement with his principal philosophical mentors—Kant and Hegel—on an issue that preoccupied him throughout his intellectual life. Although not an observant or a formally believing Jew, he was deeply engaged by questions of Jewish religious thought.[4] Guided by a

2. For an intellectual biography of Rotenstreich, see Zvie Bar-On, "Nathan Rotenstreich," in Steven T. Katz, ed., *Interpreters of Judaism in the Late Twentieth Century* (Washington D.C.: B'nai B'rith Books, 1993).

3. Rotenstreich, for instance, wrote extensively on historical consciousness. See his *Between Past and Present, An Essay on History* (New Haven: Yale University Press, 1958); and *Time and Meaning in History* (Dordrecht: Reidel, 1987). He also considered such questions with specific reference to Judaism and contemporary Israeli culture. See his *Tradition and Reality: The Impact of History on Jewish Thought* (New York: Random House, 1972), and *The Holocaust as Historical Experience: Essays and a Discussion* (New York: Holmes and Meier, 1981).

4. For a representative selection in English of his essays on Jewish thought, see his *Essays in Jewish Philosophy in the Modern Era*, ed. by Reiner Murk and introduced by Paul Mendes-Flohr (Amsterdam: Gieben, 1996). Also see his *Jewish Philosophy in Modern Times: From Mendelssohn to Rosenszweig* (New York: Holt, Reinhart & Winston, 1968).

profound respect for the teachings and values of the tradition, he was intrigued by the cognitive claims of faith. It was his conviction that philosophers—and not only Kant and Hegel—failed to appreciate the unique status of these claims. Born after a long gestation, the reflections in this volume represent Rotenstreich's attempt to meet what he considered the fundamental desideratum of philosophical discourse: to provide a sustained and systematic analysis of the cognitive horizons of faith.

To identify the cognitive specificity of faith, Rotenstreich posits that it is a sui generis phenomenon. As such, it is not to be identified with other phenomena such as religion, theology, ethics, or mysticism. The tendency to treat faith as an aspect or expression of such phenomena, Rotenstreich contends, is fundamentally flawed, for it confuses faith with its historical manifestations. Similarly, faith is not to be reduced to given experiences and emotions, for those that accompany faith are multiple and often contradictory. Faith must be understood in its own terms, independent of its various and varied historical, emotional, and experiential expressions.

As a sui generis phenomenon, Rotenstreich argues, faith is best understood as a unique attitude or orientation toward the world and reality. Here he seems to follow Martin Buber, with whom he studied at the Hebrew University. Buber regarded faith as a *Haltung*, a German word designating both an attitude and a posture, or, more precisely, a way of "holding" oneself as one encounters the world.[5] In order to identify the cognitive "essence" of this attitude, Rotenstreich adopts a phenomenological method. Accordingly, he employs the terms introduced by Edmund Husserl to distinguish the aspect of consciousness that is a mental act of intending to perceive something—in this case the attitude of faith—and the intended object of this act—here, a transcendent realm or being (and the two are not the same, as Rotenstreich repeatedly emphasizes). The former, the act of intending, Husserl called *noesis*; the latter, the object of that act, *noema*. Within the ambit of its *noesis* and *noema*, Rotenstreich observes, faith has a paradoxical

---

5. Cf. the opening sentence of Buber's *I and Thou*, which in German reads: "Die Welt ist dem Meschen zwiefältig nach seiner zwiefältigen Haltung. . . ." The I-Thou attitude (*Haltung*) is for Buber the ground of true faith.

nature. In its noetic moment it makes the implicit or explicit cognitive claim that empirical reality is incomplete and not ultimate, while in its noemetic moment it affirms "something beyond observation" and rational argument. This paradox endows faith with the peculiar epistemological status of making cognitive claims, while not being "knowledge proper." Hence, because of its cognitive, albeit sui generis nature, Rotenstreich concludes, faith cannot be identified with the absurd or the irrational.

Rotenstreich refers to faith as an "awareness"—a term he apparently also borrowed from the lexicon of Husserl, who spoke of *Anschauung,* by which he sought to denote a "direct awareness," a seeing or intuition of the essences of phenomena. Rotenstreich uses the term to mark the sui generis nature of faith as a cognitive stance that is not quite knowledge. His use of the term also seems to capture the "self-reflexive" and "self-interpretative" character of faith. Attached to the absolute or transcendent ground of truth, faith is aware of itself and its inherent paradoxes.

Rotenstreich casts a wide canvas—philology, etymology, theological docrines of theistic and nontheistic religions, as well as the reflections of various philosophers on faith. From this perspective he culls the insights upon which he constructs his characterization of the essence of faith as a universal attitude. His use of historical examples—or, as he puts it, "the historical manifestations of faith"—deserves comment. His many references to the positions and doctrines of historical religions are not adduced as empirical evidence, from which general statements about faith may be abstracted. True to the phenomenological method he employs, he does not seek to make such empirical arguments. Rotenstreich's intention is the very opposite: he wishes to show the folly and pitfalls of relying on historical material alone in describing the essence of faith. Hence, he invokes the example of Islam—which stresses "self-dedication to God more than love"—to dispute the phenomenologist Max Scheler's contention, based on the evidence of Christianity, that the essence of faith is to love. "It is necessary to consider the historical variations of faith," Rotenstreich explains, "in attempting to determine its essence and to delineate the systematic possibility of arriving from this essence to its variations.

In this methodical and systematic exposition of the essence of faith as a distinct phenomenon or mode of awareness, Rotenstreich also delineates its "various, universal components": a conjecture or leap regarding the ultimate, transcendent source of truth and meaning, trust, confidence, and an affirmation of the ultimate goodness of existence.

Although Rotenstreich died before he could complete this volume, he did manage to write a preface, the dating of which indicates that it was his very last project. He may even have realized it would be. In the last year of his life, he worked diligently to finish writing what was to remain a rough draft of the book. In the preface he makes special mention of Hayim Goldgraber, who served as his administrative assistant at the Israel Academy of the Sciences and Humanities. Upon Rotenstreich's death, Mr. Goldgraber took it upon himself to make arrangments for the publication of this manuscript, which required the tedious labor of organizing and attempting to put the fragmentary manuscript into coherent form. Without Mr. Goldgraber, who accompanied the project from its very inception, and his intelligent and indefatigable efforts this volume would not have come to realization. It was Mr. Goldgraber who invited me to undertake the editing of this manuscript. I accepted with alacrity, acknowledging that it would be a fitting opportunity for me to honor the memory of an exemplary colleague and dear friend.

The manuscript I received from Mr. Goldgraber was a work in progress, and thus essentially a draft. My task was to tighten the text and to fill in unintelligible ellipses; I introduced stylistic refinements only when they were absolutely necessary for the sake of clarity. Otherwise I sought to retain as much as possible Rotenstreich's distinctive diction and philosophical voice. Hence occasional passages remain fragmentary and others may be excessively dense, especially when such passages contain thoughts that amplify other more developed sections of Rotenstreich's exposition.

What was at times an exasperating task was rendered sweet by the support and exceptionally intelligent guidance of David Brent, senior editor at the University of Chicago Press. Mr. Brent read the manuscript several times with the eye of both a conscientious editor and a fellow philosopher. With exemplary attention to detail and philosophical nuance, he alerted me to passages that required further elucidation, and with eminent grace and tact suggested how the text should be properly understood. I and the readers of this volume are in his profound debt.

Paul Mendes-Flohr
Jerusalem
May 1997

PREFACE

The two terms used most frequently in the present study are "attitude" and "phenomenon," both of which refer to faith. The two terms are not identical or synonymous: faith as an "attitude" describes a posture or a position, whereas faith as a "phenomenon" denotes cognition as occurrence, though not through the senses, in the original connotation of the term. Faith as a phenomenon in this sense may be a point of departure for an attempt to analyze its essence. This meaning of the concept leads to a phenomenological investigation in the broad sense of the term, pointing to *Wesensschau* for the act of intuiting essences and essential relations and correspondingly to some structural components of essence. Dealing with the phenomenon of faith, one is bound to take into consideration its essence and historical manifestations, whereas the question whether religion is the essence of faith or its necessary manifestation is an open question.

I wish to thank my colleague Professor Aviezer Ravitzky for his comments on the draft of the manuscript, which prompted me to reformulate some parts of it. Ms. Mira Reich edited the manuscript. Ms. Helena Flusfeder worked with me on preparing the manuscript in its different versions. Mr. Hayim Goldgraber assisted me in his usually selfless and ever resourceful manner. I am grateful to all of them.

Nathan Rotenstreich

CHAPTER ONE

The Approach

We shall be concerned with a philosophical exposition of the essence of faith. This attempt cannot disregard the fact that the great philosophical systems scarcely dealt with the phenomenon of faith at all. To be sure, Plato and Aristotle employ the term *theologia*, but that term is meant to emphasize the position of God as the highest object or realm of philosophical cognition. Accordingly, the term *theologia* is synonymous with what became known as "metaphysics." So from the point of view of the mode of cognition, the great philosophical literature presented contemplation as an adequate mode or *epopteia* and thus brought it to prominent focus, that is, *theoria*. Hence, in the great philosophical systems we find correlation between seeing and the highest object. There is no attempt to deal with faith proper.

Faith can be integrated into the scope of philosophical discourse by an overarching approach, namely, that philosophy is concerned with basic data, either from the point of view of the attitude toward them or from the point of view of the essence and position of the data as such. Therefore, faith can be considered an attitude that cannot be subsumed under attitudes like cognition or perception, though these attitudes inform faith. The approach formulated here is guided by the attempt to articulate and to expose the particular attitude defining faith. Therefore, for the sake of this exposition, I isolate faith from other cognate phenomena, even from religion, in spite of the established connection and affinity between the two. Still, we cannot disregard the fact that faith can be presented as an attitude, while religion is a structure and even an institution. In addition, religion, in its historical manifestation of course, is a multifaceted phenomenon with endless varieties, whereas faith can be dealt with in its singular character. From this point of view, faith or piety as an attitude is a phenomenon related to individuals, while religion as an institution is essentially communal.

Since there is certainly a proximity or affinity between the two phenomena, faith and religion, I frequently "borrow" from religious concepts, which can shed light on faith. Like any other attitude, the attitude of faith is an intentionality, and an intentionality refers to a subject matter—an object, or a *noema*. Hence, in faith we discern the correlation between intentionality (*noesis*) and its object (*noema*). Thus, religious faith focuses on an object, and the most prominent object is a divine entity. Still, we presuppose the primacy of the attitude vis-à-vis communal structures, historical settings, and institutions since the attitude of faith is deemed to have a special character and can therefore absorb in itself different components, such as cognition and the motivation of one's conduct. There is a basic element in faith that allows it to be open to absorb other elements, because faith, though a given attitude, transcends itself due to its relation to its *noema,* or object. As a self-transcending attitude, we have to distinguish between faith, which is not a habit or a set pattern of behavior, and religion, which either is a habit or at least gives rise to habits. Religious formulations can be absorbed into faith, but in that absorption faith still maintains its characteristic features.

⋆ ⋆ ⋆

Though I consider components or aspects within the essence of faith, I cannot reach the conclusion, as was done in the Middle Ages, that faith seeks the intellect. The element of cognition inherent in faith does not warrant the conclusion that faith desires a partnership with intellect, that it aspires to know, assuming that knowledge in this sense is outside faith. My emphasis is on the cognitive element in faith and not on cognition outside it, though a systematic philosophical exposition is bound to deal with cognition as a phenomenon on its own. In faith we may already discern intentionality imbued with affirmation of its object as well as reverence toward that object, and we cannot assume that these two components of the attitude of faith are synonymous. Hence, in faith proper we find several components, and any exposition of them is bound to raise the question of the relation between these components or of the shift from one of them to another. The concept or term *theologia*, as mentioned before, is synonymous with metaphysics. I must mention, at least briefly, that theology did not remain a synonym of metaphysics and became a discipline meant not only to expose the essence of faith and religions but also to justify the validity of religion. The difference between articulation or exposition and validation is relevant for the approach presented here. In a sense, we justify faith by showing its singularity, but we do not justify cognitively the affirmations of faith. Moreover, faith as a singular attitude does not call for a validation, precisely because it is faith. The introduction of the approach of justification, so significant in medieval philosophy, is already an indication that faith is dealt with in a broad spectrum of approaches, and as such it is understood as calling for justification or is in need of it. Here too, perhaps, the shift from faith to religion is significant because what are justified theologically are explicit concepts of religion like God and his attributes, the creation of the world, providence, and so forth. The continuity from the classic employment of the term *theologia* to the notion of *theologia* in the Middle Ages is probably grounded in the fact that both uses are concerned with an immobile object. Thus the interpretation of that object as God could be considered a sacred doctrine, or *de divinitate ratio*. To be sure, though I emphasize some differences within historical approaches to faith and religion, we should also be aware of the similarities that exist. Hence, the presentation in this book moves from an articulation of faith as such to some specific religious concepts.

As far as religion is concerned, within this general framework we have to note also that there is a discipline, the science of religion, that entails the comparative study of religions. Since religions are taken to be historical phenomena and, thus, of different structures and institutions, their study either leads to a comparative overview or takes advantage of that overview in order to explore this or that religion as a historical datum.

In consonance with the philosophical approach guiding this study, I will thus first attempt to characterize faith as a sort of cognition that is not identical with cognition as knowledge proper, let alone science.

CHAPTER TWO

The Phenomenon of Faith

The following analysis will show that we cannot start with even a tentative description or definition of the phenomenon of faith. A definition, if formulated at all, might result from the analysis but cannot be its point of departure. I shall therefore begin by referring to the etymological root of the term "faith" and terms close to it in different languages.

Faith derives from the Latin *fides* and it is also close to the Greek *pistis.* It originally connoted surmising or conjecturing, but also trusting. As such it does not refer to a perception or to a definite knowledge, and certainly not to cognition in the logical sense of that term. Mention may be made here of the Hebrew term *emunah,* which became the common term in the various Hebrew expressions for what is described as faith. Interestingly enough, Deuteronomy (32:4) refers to God, using the term *emunah,* which by its attribution to God cannot be understood as a human attitude. It may be translated as "faithfulness" or "trustworthiness," that is to say, God of faithfulness, and without iniquity. The connotation seems to be that God is constancy untouched by any fault. In the Epistle to the Corinthians (2:22), it is said that the food of the spirit is love, joy, peace, and forbearance; then follow goodness and faith. We notice here that faith is placed among different attitudes of the human spirit and can be seen as one of the virtues, that is, one of several virtues. Here, it probably has the connotation of trust, of giving credence, but it is not a superior virtue or even a primary one.

A component of guess or conjecture is also inherent in faith, as is suggested by the terms "divination" or "to divine," which connote not just a guess, but a good guess. What should be stressed here is that the good guess becomes prominent in connection with the root word "divine"; in other words, when human beings entertain a well-warranted guess, the divine spirit is somehow present in them or active in that particular guess.

★   ★   ★

What I have thus far said about faith and its etymological root applies also to the parallel term "belief," which in scholarly opinion is etymologically close to the German *Glaube,* connoting trust, reliance, mental acceptance of a proposition, and the like. When belief is understood as trust in God, it is more than an acceptance of a proposition or an assent to a reality; it is a combination of acceptance of a reality and of trust in it. In any event, both faith and belief connote assent to something beyond observation. The employment of these different terms in the sphere of the attitude of faith in the stricter sense, that is, the religious meaning of the term, seems to be related to the position of faith and belief as an attitude of referring to something that is not perceived and cannot be perceived but can still contain the element of assertion and credence. It is neither immediate awareness nor proposition, nor is it an attitude grounded in proof. The component of hope, as we find it for instance in the Bible, belongs to this context.

It should be emphasized that a diviner is understood as a seer, a person capable of foretelling events; hence the soul is understood as divining and in this sense is prescient. This ambiguous position of faith or belief probably led Kant on the one hand to evaluate belief or faith in relation to acts of practical interest and, on the other, to list it as one of the modes of the attitude of holding a thing to be true or of subjective validity. This attitude has three degrees: opining, believing, and knowing. Thus, for Kant, believing is our considering judgment as only subjectively sufficient. At the same time, it is taken as objectively insufficient.[1]

But this evaluation of believing, placing it between opining and knowing, already implies a comparison of the attitude of conviction with other attitudes. When we are dealing with faith or belief, however, we have to be aware of the position without assuming any comparative attitude and try to discern the particular features of that position. These features are related to conjecture, while that attitude in turn is grounded in the awareness that we are holding a position or a view not based either on perception or on the syllogistic act of drawing logical conclusions.

From this point of view we can say that the possible shift of the term to the sphere that can be broadly designated as religious is rooted in that position of belief. Here a step has been taken from faith or belief to what may be described as fear or as a conjunction between fear and reverence. The German term *Ehrfurcht* is significant for reverence and awe because it combines not only an attitude of conjecture but also a specific response on the part of human beings. That response is borne by an awareness of both the distance between human beings and that which they revere and of the relationship between the two. In addition, conjecture is probably related to the component of mystery attributed to the reality of the being venerated in the religious attitude. In a more explicit religious attitude, that mystery is interpreted as the ultimate one.

Let us refer here to the term "religion," though there is still a controversy about its original meaning. One interpretation refers to the attitude of binding, which may connote undertaking a duty. That interpretation already leads us to an understanding of faith as given acts or deeds. If this is so, then, once again, faith as conjecture is to be understood as akin to deeds and not to cognition. Still, the component of cognition or awareness is present even if dimly so because conjecture is an attitude cognizant of a certain direction, though not of knowing in the strict sense of the term. To be

1. Immanual Kant, *Kritik der reinen Vernunft* (1781), B, p. 850; trans. Norman Kemp Smith as *Critique of Pure Reason* (NewYork: St. Martin's Press, 1965), p. 646.

bound to the sense that one's being is under a command of duty implies a certain form of knowledge.

I have touched on these shades of meaning in order to emphasize that the attitude of faith or belief is originally a conjunction of different attitudes. One of the major issues related to the religious attitude is that conjunction and the explication of it, or the explication by way of emphasizing this or that component. This will be the next step. The open question is whether any explication can come to grips with the variety of components inherent in faith.

CHAPTER THREE

Denominators

In the introductory exposition I placed faith in a field of association; I attempted a preliminary description of its characteristic features. Such an approach is by definition an identification of the phenomenon. In moving now to a further attempt to characterize faith, I follow a more phenomenological approach; that is to say, I try to identify the core or essence of the phenomenon. Within this context I distinguish between different approaches to such a characterization. The method of connecting the phenomenon with a denominator will be more analytical than in the previous description, and thus more philosophical. Since various interpretations of that essence are present in terms of the suggested denominator, I take the position that these identifications can be delineated by way of a graded scale. That scale does not connote an evaluation, however. But since I start with what is less cognitive and go on to what is more so, I place these different analyses on an ascending scale related to the component of cognition. Hence, feeling, a prominent feature of faith, will be seen as an attitude or as a response without cognition.

Feeling

Observe first that the component of conjecture or surmise present in *fides* contains a cognitive element, whereas the presentation of faith as feeling is deliberately less imbued with a cognitive element than what has already been presented.

In the first place, what is a feeling, and how can it be transposed to the sphere of faith? It is obvious from the various uses of the word "feeling" that it sometimes amounts to emotions, passions, or sentiments, that it is related to impressions or is a response to impressions. It has a connotation of immediate response; that is, we are impressed by something, and we respond to that impression immediately, at least from the point of view of sequence in time. We receive an impression and take it to be pleasant or unpleasant, evoking sorrow or delight. The position of feeling has been asserted as inherent in the act of touching—for instance, touching hardware or touching a table. Thus, the encounter is direct, and its response, however it is described, is also direct. In addition, as we know—and this already has a negative implication in terms of cognition—feelings have been understood as confused thinking. Without advancing any value judgment, we could say that, since faith is a phenomenon containing various facets or components, it can be viewed as confused thinking. Yet that confusion can be seen in a positive way, precisely because it is nonmethodical and many elements are involved in it. From the point of view of faith, the receptivity inherent in feeling or feelings can be understood to be significant because receptivity implies a relation to something that is beyond the feeling person. Thus, it may be understood as a response to something outside or beyond the person. These various aspects of feeling already point to one possible conclusion, namely, that placing faith on the level of feeling or feelings is far from being unambiguous, precisely because of the various possible interpretations of the act or position of feeling. We can add that sometimes the emphasis is laid on feeling as pointing to oneself and therefore to one's mood, or that feeling is a response to a situation not necessarily identified or even described. More philosophically, there have been attempts to present morality as related to feelings or sentiments, where feelings are understood as inclinations and the like.

* * *

The noncognitive character of feelings seems to be the basic point in any attempt to interpret faith as grounded in feelings. Thus,

Hume, for instance, understood belief as a peculiar feeling or sentiment, though it is not certain that he had in mind belief in its religious sense. Pascal should be mentioned in this context because he proclaims the duality of the heart and reason, saying that the heart, and not reason, experiences God and that the heart has an understanding that reason does not know. (I shall return later to the notion of experience.) Since feeling has this broad connotation as a mood related to a situation, it has sometimes been understood as one's self-forgetting and, in a more idyllic way, as a fulfillment that lacks reflection.

When we come to a more specific interpretation of faith as related or grounded in feeling, it is apposite to refer to Schleiermacher.[1] I am, of course, referring here to what is a conscious philosophical interpretation, and we are no longer reliant on some common understanding of faith. The noncognitive aspect is stressed by Schleiermacher when he says that the meaning of a religious communication is not to be looked for in books the way other concepts and cognitions are (p. 113). The rejection of books, which for Schleiermacher epitomize something given and thus mediated, is expressed even more strongly when he claims that that a person has religion who does not believe in holy scriptures, indeed, does not need any holy scriptures and could well do without them (p. 77). Hence in faith, the reference is to an unmediated relation to the infinite or to the universe (p. 75). The question arises, though it is not explicitly formulated, of how one can have an unmediated relation to something that is infinite. One could say that there is an immediate relation between a phenomenon and something that is beyond its boundaries. But the reference to the infinite or to the universe is already a cognitive interpretation of what is immediately given. To relate to something beyond the person who feels the relation does not as such warrant the identification of the frame of reference as infinite. This question applies also to another statement by Schleiermacher, that to a person of faith everything is a miracle, that is to say, something unexplained

---

1. Friedrich Daniel Ernst Schleiermacher, *Über die Religion: Reden an die Gebildeten unter ihren Verachtern,* ed. Otto Braun (Leipzig: Meiner, 1911).

and strange (p. 75). To identify something given as a miracle and to know that we cannot explain it is to assume an attitude that goes beyond feeling itself. These critical comments on Schleiermacher's "immediate" character of faith are meant to indicate that the identification of faith with feeling contains some inherent problems.

This is stressed even more definitely when the relation between feeling and intuition (*Anschauung*) is emphasized, reminding us of the well-known statement by Kant about perceptions and concepts, that intuition without feeling is blind and cannot have either the right origin or the right power; but feeling without intuition is empty. Both, as Schleiermacher notes, are there and therefore something only when and because they are originally one phenomenon and are not separated (p. 48). The component of intuition, to say the least, is already an attempt to give faith as a feeling a broad, and perhaps the broadest, possible context because intuition probably refers to infinity or to the universe, more so, at least, than feeling does. Feeling gives intuition its response by way of a human or personal sentiment, but intuition gives feeling its inherent reference to something beyond itself.

* * *

Schleiermacher himself emphasized the two corresponding aspects in the human subject, namely receptivity and activity, and of that, even more emphatically, spontaneous activity. Receptivity calls for an identification of that to which it responds or that which it receives. As Schleiermacher says, affectedness from some outside quarter is inherent in receptivity. Hence he interprets receptivity as a feeling of dependence (p. 13) without first identifying the outside dimension to which the feeling of dependence refers or that on which the person is dependent in his receptivity. The feeling of dependence is interpreted as a passive state, thus reinforcing the aspect of receptivity. In addition, it is to be noted that, since the reference to self-consciousness is essential in that exposition, Schleiermacher refers also to an Other: "In self-consciousness, there are . . . two elements: the one expresses the existence of the subject for itself, the other its co-existence with an Other" (p. 13).[2] When faith is understood as the feeling of dependence, the Other to whom or to which we relate in our feeling is that on which we are dependent and, in Schleiermacher's well-known expression, thoroughly or utterly so (the translation "absolute dependence" is not fully adequate for the German *schlechthinig*). Again, it is obvious that the formulation of thoroughgoing dependence is already an interpretation of feeling and thus cannot be understood as inherent in feeling proper as an immediate response. Thus we return to the basic issue, namely, that an attempt to identify faith as a noncognitive phenomenon par excellence cannot escape the cognitive elements, either because of its implicit vision of the universe or because of the introduction of the basic factor of dependence.

Moreover, we are aware of dependence, and to some extent at least, we interpret its impact on us as expressed in what goes by the term "power." In Paul Tillich's statement that God is the power of being in all that is, a distinction is introduced between being and the particular elements of what is, not to mention the fact that that on which we are dependent is identified as God. In other words, we introduce a basic notion or idea, and identify the being upon which we are dependent with God. After all, the description of the feeling of dependence is meant to lead us toward an identification or articulation of what goes by the term "faith" or "religious faith." The approach of identification attempts to bring traditional religious notions into its context, namely the idea of God. Hence, it is not enough that the distinction is made between receptivity and activity because activity proper is attributed to God and thus goes beyond the boundaries of human existence. The systematic conclusion that we must draw from this analysis of the noncognitive attitude as expressed in centering around feeling is that, for the sake of demystifying faith and particularly religious

2. Friedrich Schleiermacher, *The Christian Faith*, trans. H. R. Mackintosh and J. Steward (Philidelphia: Fortress Press, 1976), p. 13. Feeling and vision are taken in those interpretations of their presence in faith as ultimate elements and thus as unequivocal. This, however, is not the case, since they are differently interpreted in different religions. Consult the chapter on the structure of time in mythical and religious consciousness in E. Cassirer's *Philosophie der Symbolischen Formen*, 2: *Das mythische Denken* (Berlin: Cassirer Verlag, 1925), pp. 149 ff.

faith, we cannot remain within the boundaries of feelings. This consequence will be reinforced by an additional noncognitive or semicognitive approach to faith—namely, experience in its various meanings.

It is evident that grounding faith in feeling is a philosophical interpretation or, at least, a conceptual exposition of feeling and its direction. Even when we grant that the exposition of a phenomenon is bound to be as close as possible to that phenomenon, there is still a difference between the feeling felt and the feeling described. Still, if properly conducted, the exposition carefully avoids imposing certain qualities on the feeling described and analyzed. Moreover, one of the arguments for the reference to feeling is of a philosophical character proper because faith is conceived as a noncognitive attitude, and feeling too is conceived as a noncognitive faculty and thus may serve as the basis for faith. As we have seen, even reliance on faith cannot be sufficient because of its implicit vision of a horizon beyond itself. But vision again is taken as a noncognitive component of faith, and thus a sort of affinity is implied between the two noncognitive elements of faith—that is, feeling and vision.

* * *

Yet even from the point of view of the suggested built-in relation between feeling and faith, we should take heed of the fact that feeling in its position as a basis of faith or religion has been interpreted differently. This consideration calls for some remarks on Hegel's concept of feeling and its position in terms of faith.

Hegel says that feeling is the origin of an inner experience (p. 32).[3] He sees feeling as a simple affection of each particular subject (p. 201). The first description relates feeling to experience. What is the inherent relation between the two?

When feeling is understood as a simple affection, we are bound

---

3. G. W. F. Hegel, *Philosophische Propadeutik*, vol. 3, in *Werke*, ed. Hermann Glockner, 26 vols. (Stuttgart, 1927–1940). All unascribed citations are to Hegel and refer to the Glockner edition. A roman numeral indicates the volume number of the work cited.

to ask what that simplicity is, and indeed it is uncertain whether Hegel can maintain this description in his own presentation. In any case, when it is said that feeling is an affection of the particular subject, the problem of communication between subjects becomes central. In other words, perhaps the communication is not due to the affection as such but to that to which it refers either implicitly or explicitly. From the point of view of the essence of faith, communication is significant because, empirically or historically speaking, believing human subjects do establish modes of communication expressing their attitude.

Hegel stresses that feeling is that which is common to man and animal (p. 144).[4] He also stresses that feeling is a form containing all possible contents (p. 143). We must therefore ask whether a quality common to man and animal may be viewed as containing the potentiality of referring or absorbing any possible content. Moreover, when feeling is understood as the immediate knowledge of God (p. 131), or as the immediate unification of the gap between empirical subjectivity and the infinite thinking of the universal (p. 139), it is already an interpretation of feeling or feelings, from the point of view of the ultimate stage of human attitudes, intentionalities, or relation to the world. Religion is bound to be felt, and faith cannot be without feeling.[5] Even when feeling is the mode that indicates that something is only for myself, it is not obliterated by philosophy; instead, it is given true content through philosophy.[6] Thus Hegel introduces into the context of describing and placing feeling in its essential relation to faith his broad systematic view that there is a continuity from one stage of the relation to the world to another, including the continuous dialectical advancement from feeling to thinking and philosophical reflection.

These aspects are reinforced by Hegel's exposition of the essence of faith. He understands faith as a relation of the finite to the absolute (p. 157).[7] It is the relation constituted by speculation

---

4. *Vorlesungen über die Philosophie der Religion*, I, vol. 15.
5. *Vorlesungen über die Geschichte der Philosophie*, I, 17:368.
6. *Vorlesungen über die Philosophie der Religion*, II, 16:353.
7. *Aufsätze aus dem kritischen Journal der Philosophie*, vol. 1.

regarding the identity of the finite and the absolute, the relation of which the finite subject otherwise lacks consciousness. We can view faith from the position of the limitations of the subject but also from the position of the identity that is articulate through philosophical speculation. In classical terms, the way up and the way down coincide. Faith as such in its own boundaries retains finite and empirical reality on the one hand, and the absolute position of the infinite on the other (p. 286). No further elaboration is needed to stress that the introduction of the perspective of infinity to the description of the phenomenon of faith already oversteps the phenomenological understanding of faith, namely, by placing it in the context of a philosophical system based on, as said before, the continuity from feeling to speculation. The significance of the position of faith in the context of a system of continuity is expounded by Hegel himself, namely, that the infinite is not truth since it cannot absorb the finite in itself (p. 293). Hence the infinite in its ultimate exposition has to be presented as absorbing or, to use the technical expression, sublating (*Aufheben*) the finite. Since feeling is understood as subjective certainty of the eternal,[8] the very reference to the eternal already orients feeling or faith beyond itself. Moreover, even when faith is interpreted as subjective certainty, the notion of certainty goes beyond feeling and inheres in its awareness of its referent and self-interpretation. This is emphasized by Hegel himself when he says that the true ground of faith is the spirit.[9] Thus, starting with the affection of every particular subject, which is apparently an exposition of feeling from the position of the subject, does not prevent the grounding of faith in the spirit containing feeling, which is not an affection of the particular subject. This placing eventually leads to the understanding that the subjective spirit hears (*vernimmt*) that which is objective.[10] To be sure, faith proper lacks the consciousness that is essentially thinking.[11] Thus, faith can be understood both in its own boundaries and in the context of the articulated philosophical system.

8. *Vorlesungen über die Philosophie der Geschichte*, 11:523.
9. *Vorlesungen über die Philosophie der Religion*, I, 15:229.
10. *Vorlesungen über die Geschichte der Philosophie*, I, 17:105.
11. *Vorlesungen über die Geschichte der Philosophie*, III, 19:546.

The process or procedure of establishing continuity between these two poles constitutes a bridge between them; it is important to stress that it is a philosophical bridge, constructed not from the perspective of faith but from that of reflection.

The objective of our exposition of the different interpretations of faith by Schleiermacher and Hegel has been to show (*a*) that feeling may be interpreted differently and thus cannot be taken as the basis for the attitudes of faith or belief understood as unmediated and lacking ambiguity and (*b*) that in Hegel's system the philosophical context of the exposition of faith and feeling is more prominent than in that of Schleiermacher. I considered Hegel's conception in order to emphasize different interpretations of the essence of feelings as it pertains to faith. I shall deal with Hegel's view more extensively in the last chapter.

It is apposite to highlight at this juncture an additional aspect: feeling is a state of the soul and of the mind. Since it cannot interpret itself, if an interpretation is added, it may be one-sided. The religious interpretation of feeling, for instance, endows it with a harmonious direction. When feeling is understood as *Stimmung* (mood), it takes on a more constant character, the German term having musical or vocal nuances lacking in the English term *mood*. When feeling is interpreted as burden (*Last*), it can hardly be understood as carrying a connotation of faith. An enigmatic component can thus be understood as being inherent in feeling, even the claim that feeling the "here and now" with immediacy is an interpretation of the instantaneous aspect of feeling. From this point of view, the religious interpretation is again—to put it mildly—problematic.[12]

Remaining within the framework of denominators of faith, we shall now examine some of the variations of the interpretation of faith as experience.

Experience

The attempt to rely on a noncognitive approach also amounts to reliance on a nonconceptual approach. Experience is taken as a

---

12. Martin Heidegger, *Sein und Zeit* (Halle an der Saale: Niemeyer, 1927), pp. 134 ff.

nonconceptual encounter of data or as an approach to them without reference to proofs or to interrelated contexts. In this sense, it is a kind of continuation of the emphasis on the noncognitive essence of feelings, although, as we shall see, there is a difference between feeling and experience.

It should be noted at the start that there is ambiguity in the concept of experience in some languages—in English, "experience" stands for what in German is differentiated as *Erlebnis* and *Erfahrung*. *Erlebnis* connotes more than experience in the limited sense. It is an impression absorbed or integrated in the texture of our existence. Sometimes it connotes an event solely or particularly significant for ourselves, thus becoming part of our broader existence. Thus, *Erlebnis* connotes more an internalization of an occurrence while *Erfahrung* connotes more the encounter with something that we undergo, that we experience. When we relate faith to experience in the first sense (*Erlebnis*), we probably wish to underline the significance of faith for our existence and not the scattered encounters occurring in the course of our biography. The question will therefore be, What is the meaning of experience in the context of faith, or what goes by the name of religious experience?

⋆　⋆　⋆

When we look at the heading of one of the chapters of Rudolf Otto's book, *The Idea of the Holy*—namely, the human "creature's" feeling that is the reflex of the numinous feeling engendered by the object perceived to be beholden—we find a conjunction of so many elements that an analysis is mandatory. Furthermore, Otto refers to Schleiermacher and his "lucky exposition of the feeling of dependence."[13] In the first place, the feeling of being a creature is already an interpretation of "dependence" because a creature is not self-creating; it is a creature, that is to say, it is created. Yet there is a leap from the feeling of dependence to the feeling of being a

---

13. Rudolf Otto, *Das Heilige*, trans. John W. Harvey as *The Idea of the Holy: An Inquiry into the Non-rational Factor in the Idea of the Divine and Its Relation to the Rational* (New York: Oxford University Press, 1936), p. 8.

creature, for the term "creature" is already a generalization and, hence, a comprehensive interpretation of dependence. It presents or posits entities that, to some extent at least, are grounded in themselves by self-awareness. To be sure, we find this relation of a creature to itself in the notion of feeling of oneself, since the self is already an entity and not a scattered moment experiencing something beyond itself. The polarity of feeling of the object and the feeling of the self is again a duality that we reach by interpreting the moment of feeling as dependence. Indeed, this position is amplified by looking at feelings as a reflex of what is described as "numinous." The difference between the immediate and the interpretation of it is implied from the very beginning. Otto himself says that the presupposition of utter dependence is a feeling evoked by the utter superiority of that which is beyond the experiencing subject and which we cannot be drawn into the ambit of our feelings. Hence, confronting once again seemingly inherent ambiguities, we are obliged to address what feeling is and where experience and interpretation begin.

Paradoxical as it may sound, a kind of continuity between one component and another is inherent in Otto's conception of the numinous feeling, though it is not explicitly stressed. In addition, there are various attempts to interpret the objective sublime pole of experience as that which is tremendous, majestic, full of energy. These various aspects eventually are considered as manifestations or moments of the numinous. Significantly enough, in the numinous there are components of attraction as well as those of separation; yet the central component is still that of the *tremendum,* and thus the *tremendum* is totally removed from us. We could say that the variety of the components and even the contradiction between them is merely an exposition of the objective pole of faith. The question remains whether faith—without its exposition—can be an amorphous phenomenon or whether the exposition is essential to the very essence of faith. If so, there can be no faith without awareness. If this is the case, we overstep the realm of feeling from the very beginning.

⋆ ⋆ ⋆

The introduction of the notion of *Erlebnis* to the context of faith is problematic in itself. *Erlebnis* has been understood as identity between what is inside the person and the content that the person internalizes. This description of the essence of *Erlebnis* is problematic in itself because it somehow pretends to replace Hegel's identity of thinking and reality. Yet there is a basic difference between thinking and *Erlebnis* since the first is comprehensive or at least tries to be so. Thus, the assumed or pretended identity is understood to be the other side of the systematic character of thinking, meeting the overriding character of reality. *Erlebnis* is instantaneous and thus occurs momentarily—at the moment—and is limited by its very character and background. To employ the concept or occurrence of *Erlebnis* to faith would disregard a basic component of faith, namely that faith relates to something beyond the person even when that which is beyond evokes attachment, reverence, devotion, and any other response.

This is a step forward in the second interpretation of experience in the German sense of *Erfahrung.* Experience in this sense is understood as something achieved or arrived at and thus not as something occurring on the spur of the moment. Terminologically speaking, experience has been related to memory, and similarly as a reference to accumulated wisdom, for example, when we say "an experienced doctor," that is, a doctor who has accumulated the lesson or lessons acquired from his practice. This interpretation of experience implies the person's going out to that which surrounds him. Again, it does not point to the inner stream of one's awareness. The still problematic character of that application of the concept will become salient in our analysis of William James's *Varieties of Religious Experience.*[14]

⋆ ⋆ ⋆

With due reservations, James regards religion as "the feelings, acts, and experiences of individual men in their solitude, so far as

---

14. William James, *The Varieties of Religious Experience: A Study in Human Nature* (New York: Modern Library, 1902). All references are to this edition. The Hebrew translation of the book renders "experience" as C*havaiah*, that is, *Erlebnis*, whereas the German translation is given as *Erfahrung.*.

they apprehend themselves to stand in relation to whatever they may consider the divine" (pp. 31–32). We notice in this tentative definition that there is a basic relation or intentionality of an individual's conduct with respect to the divine, who by definition is beyond or above the individual. Hence, the reference to religious feelings and religious impulses or to the individual's mental constitution may emphasize the component of personal existence that as such is correlated to that which is outside the individual. The analysis of these aspects of religious experience is central in James's interpretation of religion.

Programmatically, he says: "The plain truth is that to interpret religion one must in the end look at the immediate content of the religious consciousness." It is because of that emphasis that psychological or even psychopathological aspects like melancholy and conversion are so central in James's exposition (p. 4). Again, the problematic character of his interpretation is manifest in his claim that "religion, whatever it is, is a man's total reaction upon life" (p. 13). But if experience is understood as psychological phenomenon, we may wonder how the notion of "total" is brought in. That which is total cannot be experienced unless we assume a kind of immersion of the partial psychological or experiential acts in the totality. If this is the case, then experience is the bridge toward this immersion, but the final stage of the process ceases to be experience and becomes unification with the totality.

This two-sided character of the religious experience is perhaps inherent to James's analysis because of the significance he attributes to the mystical states of consciousness. Accordingly, he claims that "mysticism must be faced in good earnest . . . . One may say truly, I think, that personal religious experience has its root and center in mystical states of consciousness" (p. 35). If this is so, then, historically speaking (and he is aware of this), James is close to Hegel, who thought that mysticism is the highest manifestation of religion. In this sense, we could extrapolate and say that religious awareness or experience that does not reach the peak of mysticism is but a step toward that stage. Thus, in a sense, the full manifestation of religious experience according to James himself is pantheistic and optimistic or at least the opposite of pessimistic (p. 37). To be sure, implied here is an interpretation of mysticism as inherently pantheistic. From a historical or typological view, one may question this assumption. James adds that it is antinaturalistic, but here again one may question whether this holds true for all forms of pantheism, such as that of Spinoza, for it is not at all certain whether the grades of knowledge, culminating in the intellectual love of God, necessarily imply twice-bornness (p. 413).

★   ★   ★

To some extent, James himself is more cautious about referring to the scope of faith when he says that the field of religion is so wide that no one could pretend to cover it. There is religious fear, religious love, religious awe, religious joy, and so forth (p. 413). Yet, in spite of the recognition of the varieties of religious experience—as is indicated in the very title of his book—there is an implicit superimposition of mysticism as the ultimate experience. To some extent, James wavers here between his empirical inquiry (pp. 28, 29), which guides him in the direction of identifying varieties of experience, and his attempt to present a construction of religious experience, namely, to look at mysticism as "the ideal type of that experience." In addition, we may wonder about the statement "No religion has ever yet owed its prevalence to "apodictic certainty"" (p. 254). Implied is the distance between what religious experience attempts to arrive at, namely, full certainty, and the actual point of arrival that is beyond experience. In addition, we must ask how the tentative component of apodictic certainty comes at all into the horizon of religious experience or faith. Religious experience relates to something beyond the person, or, as some critical views would say, we project the aspired certainty from the sphere of cognition to the sphere of faith. It goes without saying that the mystic or pantheistic interpretation of faith or religious experience replaces the feeling of dependence that served as a starting point of this part of our exposition. Immersion is not dependence since the former implies partialness of the person, while the latter connotes a duality between the person and the being he or she is dependent on (p. 325).

Coming back to the question of a common denominator of the religious experience, we have to conclude that religious experience as interpreted by James is to some extent based on the recognition of the plurality of components inherent in that experience. Thus, perhaps the assumption that at bottom that experience has a single denominator does not hold good. We are left, however, with the notion of experience, and a presumed affinity between faith and experience. Parallel to this, there is the assumption that religious experience attains at full realization mysticism, but faith as such would, then, cease to be present, for it would be replaced by a state of integration or union.

★   ★   ★

At this juncture, it is appropriate to make some comments on Whitehead's observations on our topic. Whitehead speaks about the particularity of things experienced (p. 69); experience is community with the data experienced (p. 123).[15] A relation apparently exists between the data that are experienced and experience as such. Hence, there are metaphoric expressions such as "vectors," since in feelings we feel what is *there* and transform it into what is *here*; this is the objective lure of feeling (p. 133). Speaking about the subjective pull of feelings, Whitehead points to the feeling individual who is the unity emergent from his or her own feelings (p. 136). We could say that the position of the feeling individual as a unity is already a step between that which is instantaneously given and that which is a kind of manifestation of an act of unification and which is the presupposition of the fragmentary feelings themselves. The duality or the correlation between feeling and that to which it refers is formulated by Whitehead in saying that the subjective form includes, as a defining element in its emotional pattern, a certain form, or eternal object (p. 408). Significantly, feeling as described here is "belief."

To be sure, Whitehead uses the term "belief" and not "faith,"

15. Alfred North Whitehead, *Process and Reality: An Essay in Cosmology* (New York: Social Science Book Store, 1941).

but this semantic difference is probably not essential. What is systematically important is that Whitehead points out the correlation between the component of feeling and what he calls the "eternal object." Hence, it is not essential for the identification of religious experience to insist on the immersion of the experience in a total reality. What is essential is the correlation and not the pantheistic interpretation as implied in James. This aspect of experience is perhaps amplified in Whitehead's terminology as "presentational immediacy";[16] that is to say, that which is immediate points to that which is beyond itself.

The well-known concept of "world loyalty"[17] is a kind of a résumé of these different discernments in Whitehead's writings. Loyalty does not amount to immersion but points to an attitude of faithfulness, of fidelity or reverence; these nuances constitute a correlation and not a unification. To be sure, we can ask whether world loyalty is applicable, for example, to Buddhism, where the world is to be annihilated as one attains Nirvana. In addition, and this is a significant tacit component, loyalty is derived from *loi* (law). That is to say, fidelity may call for self-restraint precisely because loyalty to the world is to preserve the world and, thus implicitly or explicitly, to restrain human activities in order to prevent any human attempt to become superior vis-à-vis the surrounding world. This aspect may be prominent precisely in a technological society, and here religious experience may contain a self-accepted restriction of human activities. Loyalty to the world may be not only a correlate of experience of religion but also a norm of human conduct.

World loyalty has a positive connotation of belonging to the universe as a whole; it enlarges and enhances the existence of the individual. Even the notion of Nirvana as implying the extinguishing of personal and terrestrial existence has a positive direction in its outcome as salvation. It is a release from painful existence—samsara. In the final salvation the person becomes a saint. This positive

16. Alfred North Whitehead, *Meaning and Effect* (Cambridge: Cambridge University Press, 1928), p. 17.

17. Alfred North Whitehead, *Religion in the Making* (New York: Meridian Books, 1960), p. 59.

direction differs from various metaphorical expressions, such as being shipwrecked.[18] In addition, the moral aspect of world loyalty is emphasized by Whitehead, who notes that religion in general highlights the ideal unity of the universe.[19] The notion of the ideal points to something beyond religious experience despite its varieties, even those which do not stress the inherent unity of the universe. If the world at large cannot be explained, it is even more the case in terms of the dimension of the ideal.

Affirmation

The emphasis laid on feeling as the essence of faith and the placing of faith by implication with the realm of experience perforce leads one to ignore or overlook the situation in which faith arises or takes place. The propositional component is subdued or even neglected. Since faith is an attitude or an approach to reality in the broadest sense of that term, one may wonder how that reality can find expression, if at all, in the mere impression of the believing individual or the subject.

From this point of view, Cardinal Newman in his *Grammar of Assent* deliberately introduced the propositional element into the exposition or analysis of faith or belief. I will use his term "assent," and attempt to broaden it by the term "affirmation" in order to indicate the quality of assent as containing not only propositions and their approval but also the attitude of affirming the reality expressed in informal propositions. I consider such reality as being of particular significance and not only as that which is given. We should observe again that the two terms "belief" and "faith" are present in Cardinal Newman's analysis when he says that faith in its theological sense includes a belief. Real assent is synonymous with belief (p. 89).[20] Belief is concerned with things concrete and not abstract, and the quality of exciting the mind by moral and

18. See Hans Blemenberg, *Schiffbruch mit Zuschauer*, Paradigma einer Daseinsmetapher (Frankfurt: Suhrkamp, 1979).

19. Alfred North Whitehead, *Modes of Thought* (New York: Macmillan, 1978), p. 39.

20. John Henry Cardinal Newman, *An Essay in Aid of a Grammar of Assent* (New York: Longmans, Green & Co., 1906).

imaginative properties is taken to be part of that which is apprehended by belief. This conjunction of the different attitudes has led me to employ the term "affirmation"; I shall return to that conjunction presently.

⋆ ⋆ ⋆

Our starting point lies in the distinction between different propositions, that is, the notional assent and the real one. The notional assent relates to propositions and their interrelation, while the real assent relates to propositions that stand for things (p. 90). The notional assent refers to the inner discourse and its elements, while the real assent is what we should describe in phenomenological terminology as intentionality to objects. Also, since religion or belief are of the real assent, that assent cannot be disconnected from a real person; hence, it is said that religion is personal (p. 40). The question of the paradoxical relation between that which is inherently personal and yet still refers to reality in the deepest and widest sense of the term is perhaps not raised by Cardinal Newman.

Methodologically, the propositions of belief may be placed within the framework of informal reasoning, informal reasoning refers to particular matters, which are formulated in statements of probability and not of evidence. Possibly because of this consideration, Cardinal Newman tried to establish a thematic connection between assent in his interpretation and the Aristotelian notion of *phronesis* (or in Latin *prudentia*). One may wonder whether the assumption of such an affinity is warranted since "prudence" does not refer to reality as a whole but rather to circumstances and our orientation to them, including our intentional attempt to control them. One may question whether belief or faith, informal as they are in the propositions that express them, are of a prudential character or whether they rather occupy a special place that combines, to use the traditional term, contemplation and attachment or loyalty. The informal character of the statements assessed or affirmed becomes prominent in the distinction between various modes of certainty or credence suggested by Cardinal Newman. Religious teaching contains certitude, and there is apparently a kind of synonymy between assent and certitude. It is a material certitude or an interpretative one (p. 55). Given the different terminological components, the main point is in the attempt to identify a certain mode of conviction that is meant to be characteristic of belief as a sum total of informal propositions.

Cardinal Newman takes one step further, bringing together the propositional assent and the moral direction of the person. The reasoning behind this integration of the two aspects are manifold. One is probably of a historical character, namely, that religions within the scope of this analysis are of a normative character: they guide human behavior, character, responses, and so forth. The more systematic aspect seems to lie in the assertion that there is a true parallel between human and divine knowledge (pp. 210–19). Hence, from the point of view of human knowledge, precisely because it is informal and refers to reality, the consideration of the mental state out of which assent emerges leads also to the consideration of the guiding authority of the mental state or what Cardinal Newman calls "illative sense" (p. 239). Since the integration of the ontological aspect of faith with the normative one is, as already indicated, common in religious thought, the significant point to emphasize here is the interpretation of the normative component as conscience and not as duty.

⋆ ⋆ ⋆

For Kant, duty is the core of morality, and its formulation and the acceptance of its authority do not require reference to God as legislator. On the contrary, God is understood as a full realization of morality and not as its origin.[21] Kant said therefore that morality is based on the conception of the human being as a free agent. Because human beings are free they bind themselves through their reason to unconditioned laws. Human beings do not stand in need

21. Immanuel Kant, *Die Religion innerhalb der Grenzen der reinen Vernunft,* Akademe Ausgabe, 6:3. *Religion within the Limits of Reason Alone,* trans. Theodore M. Greene and Hoyt H. Hundson (New York and Evanston, Ill.: Harper & Row, 1969), p. 3.

either of the idea or another being over them, or of an incentive other than the law itself, to do their duty. Hence, for its own sake, morality does not need religion at all. Cardinal Newman cannot accept this view because the relation to reality is an inherent, fundamental aspect of the human being's reality in the world and cannot be substituted by the notion of an autonomous human being. Moreover, human beings vis-à-vis themselves, being creatures, are characterized apparently not as following or respecting a norm but as calling themselves to order or as being judged and evaluated. Hence, conscience in this concept is the most significant element of the ethical attitude. It both commands and checks human beings in their responses and conduct. The presupposition is that, since God is the lawgiver, the human being as a creature who is the image of God is not his or her own lawgiver but the interpreter of the law given to him or her. Conscience, in the etymological sense, contains the element of cognition and thus seems more akin to the direction of assent central to Cardinal Newman's analysis. To be sure, conscience can never be of a formal or syllogistic character, though it may apply rules to specific events or responses and circumstances. In any case, this conception attempts to bring together the affirmative aspect of belief or faith, implied by the point of view asserting a given reality, and the acceptance of ethical obligation.

*   *   *

The issue at stake is whether the nonformal propositional aspect of faith does justice to the particular essence of that phenomenon. The juxtaposition with formal statements is only the broad frame of reference, and the question remains open as to whether it presents the specific difference of faith or belief. I have already indicated that it is not enough to speak of informality because of the universal or comprehensive essence of that to which informal propositions, credence, and so forth refer. They are not within the horizon of experience, let alone feeling, and not even informal propositions. Methodologically, we here face an attempt to find a context in which faith or belief may be placed and, therefore, dealt with. Yet the question remains whether that context is to be understood only as a bridge enabling us to formulate analogies or whether it is a common denominator of faith as such. Even the search for a common denominator cannot render us oblivious to the specific and essential character of faith. The attempt to place religion within the structure of a philosophical system, and thus of reason, only underscores this difficulty.

The approaches criticized do not content themselves with a phenomenological approach to faith but move willy-nilly to some sort of construction with the view of connecting exposition with justification—although from the point of view of acts pertaining to human consciousness. The issue is whether such a construction can be avoided at all or, at least, whether the philosophical expositions of faith should be, indeed, expositions and consciously not constructions. This comment leads us to one further step in our examination of faith, namely, an attempt to relate it to components that initially are not peculiar to it and thus function as denominators whether it is formulated this way or not.

System and Reason

The attempt, on the one hand, to identify the core of faith by relating it to a common denominator of all possible expressions of faith—which has a meaning in itself—leaves us with the question whether such an attempt can do justice to the specific qualities of faith as a phenomenon and also whether any common denominator is adequate to elucidating the essence of the phenomenon. On the other hand, an attempt to place faith within a specific system precludes the possibility of finding the desired denominator because a system is by definition a structure of different elements or spheres. Thus, when considered within the structure of a system, faith must, at least programmatically, not be reduced to or included within the terms of the system, that is, its essential elements, such as feeling, experience, or whatever.

This observation leads us to an analysis of Hermann Cohen's endeavor to place the concept of religion within a philosophical system. Let us observe at the outset that Cohen is dealing with religion and not with faith per se, and this in itself calls for a more detailed analysis. When Cohen refers to faith, he refers to its principles, which may be compared with the principles of reason;[22] religion is bound to truth.[23] It establishes a particular concept of God as well as its own concept of human being, and here again the issue at stake is religion. Within the context of the system, Cohen even uses the expression "systematic religion";[24] there is an inner relation between the true religion and the truth of systematic philosophy. Systematic philosophy is the doctrine of the unity of the human being in his or her modes of creating culture (p. 136). If this is so, and philosophy is expressed in the creation of culture, religion must be incorporated into the system of philosophy not only because of the concepts it employs but also because of its effect on human culture. In this sense culture becomes the broadest common realm of human creativity in which we can discern some particularities without losing sight of the central point established by the system of philosophy.

The immanence of philosophy in all the major directions of culture (p. 9) is the universal presupposition of Cohen's approach. Because of that approach, we must investigate religion's position in his system of philosophy and thus the relation between religion and what can be called the established spheres of a Kantian philosophical system—that is, cognition, ethics, and aesthetics—to which Cohen added his own interpretation of psychology. If we compare Cohen's interpretation of the structure of the philosophical system, when he deals with religion, against those philosophical views that do not consider religion to be a specific sphere, his principle of origin (*Ursprung*) is central in this context; origin and creation are interrelated. Reason as understanding in the broad sense of cognition is grounded in the principle of origin and makes that principle manifest. Nothing is given to reason, that is to say

22. Hermann Cohen, *Der Begriff der Religion im System der Philosophie* (Giesen: Toppelmann, 1915), p. 107.

23. Hermann Cohen, *Religion der Vernunft aus den Quellen des Judentums* (1919), p. 45. *Religion of Reason out of the Sources of Judaism*, trans. Simon Kaplan with an introductory essay by Leo Strauss (New York: Ungar Publishing Co., 1972), pp. 11 ff.

24. Cohen, *Der Begriff der Religion im System der Philosophie*, p. 122.

that whatever is present in its sphere is created by reason itself. Kant's notion of spontaneity here becomes most prominent or most radically expressed. Hence, being is not something to be deciphered let alone given to reason; being is the being of thinking. Therefore, thinking as thinking of being is thinking or cognition (p. 15). It is, therefore, mistaken to assume that something is given to thinking; thinking is its own origin and the objects of its thought are "spontaneously" created in thinking. Guided by reason, thinking spans origin and creation (p. 81).

The concern with religion leads Cohen to a different interpretation of the position of being, namely, the identification of being with the uniqueness of God or the identity of God with being; that is to say, vis-à-vis that identity, no other being remains valid (p. 26). God makes himself valid as being (p. 20). Cohen apparently assumes that the ontological position of God cannot be disregarded when the phenomenon of religion is considered. Hence, the first step he takes in the direction of identifying the specific essence of religion is what may be called the ontologization of the direction of the philosophical system, although its other spheres— with some reservations about ethics—do not incorporate this ontological direction. To be sure, Cohen does not deal with the question of the relation between the ontological dimension and the lack of it, amounting to the spontaneity of reason, at least not in any detail. This may be due to a major issue attendant to facticity of reason, to which I shall soon refer.

* * *

Yet religion is characterized not only by the position of God in terms of being but also by the position of man that is the concern of the moral or ethical element inherent in the religious attitude. Two aspects should be emphasized in this context. The first is the relation between God and the human being as a person: the human being, too, has to be preserved, and this, according to Cohen, is the ultimate significance of religion (p. 134). Cohen attempts to base this correlation between the position of God and that of human being in the broader conception of the relation between the idea and its appearance when he says that every idea demands the correlate of its appearance (p. 53). This correlation is that between the infinite and the finite (p. 134), and thus it is the correlation between God as being in the proper sense of that notion and human beings who are appearances in two senses. Human beings manifest the position of being created by God and thus are correlated to him, but they also present or represent the humaneness of human beings. The humaneness is the essence, while human beings are appearances, and in this context there is a self-development of human beings toward humanity (p. 53).

Here again there seems to be a breakthrough in the direction of ontology, not only on the level of God as the being par excellence but also on the level of the empirical—individual—human beings. In order to maintain the correlation between God and human beings, Cohen thought he had to introduce into the context normative human behavior, that is, consideration for individual human beings, and not only consideration for universal humanity that would lead to the conception that individual human beings are representatives of humanity and do not have a self-contained status of their own.

It is essential to ask why Cohen brought up the position of individual human persons in relation to the essence of religion. He seems to have thought that the philosophical ethics formulated by Kant refers to humanity as a whole and thus tends to disregard the status of individual human beings. However, since it refers to the universality of moral law, it refers to the universality of humankind, leading to a correaltion between these two aspects of universality. Yet Cohen did not attempt to supplement the universal direction of ethics by integrating consideration for every individual into it. He took the view that this consideration is inherently present in religion, and as such it must be regarded as pertaining to religion, without leading to a new formulation of philosophical ethics. Religion is thus a formulation of a systematic specificity that cannot be dissolved outside itself in any sphere of the system.

The empirical aspect of human beings' individuality leads Cohen to the formulation that the God of the individual is the God of religion (p. 101). Hence, at least initially, religion is concerned with the sins of concrete individuals (p. 77). Again, we may ask here, beyond the historical connections, what the relation or even affinity is between religion and sin—unless indeed we assume that human beings are in need of being forgiven and therefore cannot overcome their sins within their own realm, let alone reach a level of purification from sin.

The notion of sin immediately points to the religious interpretation. Notice here the inclusion of empirical aspects in the sphere of religion, though Cohen does not stress this characterization when he speaks about longing as related to God, associating the concept of the God of salvation with that of the God of longing. These two attributes situate God as the God of the individual. We somehow remain uncertain as to whether the introduction of this characterization to the sphere of the religion of reason is justified, even more so when these components are said to establish religion. Again, the question arises as to whether Cohen did not try to incorporate elements traditionally connected with religious views or more specifically with historical religions into the philosophical interpretation of religion.

The issue is significant because Cohen was not satisfied with the articulation of some implicit elements in faith or in the religious outlook. He tried to transpose them from historical religions to a systematic presentation of religion. Because of this, the issue of the justification for such a transposition becomes essential. Philosophy appears here not only as an interpretation of religion from within but also as imposing concepts on the philosophical system that do no emerge out of its structure. To put it differently, Cohen did not confine himself to situating the notion of being or even of the correlation between being and its appearance; instead, he moved in the direction of imbuing the realm of appearance with many detailed concepts or aspects that go beyond the architectonic relation between true being and its appearance. Thus Cohen went not only beyond the notion of spontaneity and origin in acknowledging being but also beyond what can be called the "essence" of human being to some of human being's particularities. We shall now consider another central issue in Cohen's philosophy, namely, the position of reason proper, where the religious interpretation and the philosophical systematization are meant to coincide.

★   ★   ★

Here Cohen goes either outside the system or beyond it. He already does this in interpreting givenness as being dependent on the giver—that is, God. Reason in its inner structure endows the human being as an entity of reason and, thus, as a correlate of God to revelation. Since the human being is a creature of God, the human being's reason conditions the relation of reason to God. Creation is the logical consequence of the status of the being of God as unique. When revelation is considered as a continuation of creation, it leads to the consequence that the presence of reason is also a continuation of creation. Directed to human beings, it becomes the presupposition of the human being's cognition. That cognition becomes manifest in the knowledge of good and evil, that is, in ethical knowledge. Cohen does not imply the heteronomous character of morality since he is not dealing here with norms as such but with the very possibility of being guided by norms. Thus, he is concerned with the creation of human beings specifically in the creation of their reason.

The presupposition of this conception seems to lie in Cohen's attempt to combine several elements in exploring the essence of religion. In the first place, he wants to establish, confirm, and justify the unique position of the human being within the created universe. Because of that endeavor, he moves toward the establishment of a particular relationship between God and human beings. As long as we are dealing with creation as a whole, that particular relation cannot be discerned because creation as a religious category applies to the world as a whole and does not contain a particularity in terms of the human being's position and his or her essence. Cohen tries to introduce an additional component of religion: that the human being is created as an image of God; that is to say, on the one hand the human being possesses a particular essence, and, on the other, this essence connotes a particular affinity between the human being and God. Hence, the human being's endowment with reason is a particular act of creation but, by the same token, a revelation. It is clear at this juncture that Cohen brings together several traditional religious concepts and attempts to consider them as constituting a consistent structure.

The correlation between the human being and God is a two-way relation: God creates the human being as a special being or creature within the broad context of the universe. Human beings relate to God mainly because they—and only they—are endowed with reason, though what aspects of faith are expressed in the direction of human being's relation to God is not clear. One expression of the relation to human being is apparently the position of the human being as an empirical reality. God is being in its purity, and therefore the correlated dimension in the human sphere is the position of human beings as real beings established as individuals and not submerged in a universal context or realm, for example, humanity. To be sure, Cohen does not justify that direction of correlation from pure being to empirical existence by way of a conceptual correlation because he introduces the ethical aspect into his deliberation, namely, that only the empirical human being can be recognized in his pain or even sin. One could argue that the introduction of the concept of sin echoes components of the religious conception from the very beginning because sin is not just a transgression of norms but implies defiance of the divine imperative.

Systematically, Cohen tried at this juncture to introduce an ethical component, which is religiously grounded not only textually or historically but also conceptually. Since he had before him Kant's interpretation of ethics—namely, the reference to humanity as such and concurrently to human beings as representatives of humanity—he attempted to supplement that interpretation of ethics by stressing the position of individual human beings who are not only representatives but beings of a singular character or position as well. The ontological component of human existence is accompanied by the ethical position of individuals who are ontologically particular and partners of a relationship based on empathy, sympathy, and forgiveness. In this context, religion or faith is the reservoir of notions that supplement the ethical system apparently without clashing with it, precisely because they are a supplementary and not a competing interpretation of human existence and its moral connotation. Yet, because of the introduction of this connotation, the correlation of God and the human being bound to be confined to the ontological aspect, while the ethical one is limited to the human sphere and cannot have an adequate correlate in the divine realm.

An additional issue in Cohen's philosophy of religion we must consider is what he calls the creation of the human being in reason. The implication seems to be that creation is not confined to the very presence of human beings in the universe. It goes further to the particularity of human beings in terms of their ethical capacity, and not only in terms of the interrelation between them. The creation of human beings is described by Cohen as a logical consequence of the unique being of God (p. 100)—and we may wonder about the meaning of that *logical* consequence.

Is the creation of human beings—endowed with reason—a consequence as in a syllogism, or is the uniqueness of the being of God the precondition for the creation of man in reason, but not a logical consequence? The same query applies to a different rendering, namely that God's being, vis-à-vis human beings, is a presupposition for cognition. But that presupposition implies that human beings are created in the image of God, and thus their secondary position, if I may call it that, is expressed in their being endowed with reason as the broadest ground of cognition and, further still, that cognition is one of good and evil. Thus Cohen tries to ground the ethical dimension of interhuman relations in cognition, which in turn presupposes the being of God. But this is apparently not enough because of the further attempt to bring together the correlation and the reciprocity between human being and God. Because of reason, the human being becomes subjectively the discoverer of God (p. 103); or, as it were, the being of God becomes actual only in the cognition of the human being (pp. 103, 144; pp. 85 ff.).[25] To be sure, in order to recognize the position of God, awareness, understanding, or reason at large are necessary.

---

25. Cohen, *Religion der Vernunft aus den Quellen des Judentums.*

Yet awareness is not only the recognition of being but also the actualization of the divine status within the human orbit. It is possible that Cohen was aware of the paradoxical position of awareness in relation to the independent and self-contained divine entity since it is through reason that we become aware of our relation or even correlation with God. Without our awareness, God would remain, to put it strongly, an opaque reality. Hence, Cohen says that through reason both creation and revelation come to fulfillment (p. 103; p. 85). If this is so, then Cohen is aware, without stressing it in so many words, of the inherent paradox of faith: faith refers to God, being dependent on human being. But without faith there would be no relation to God or acknowledgment of his reality. Acknowledgment becomes a central issue, but it can be achieved only from the position and perspective of human being. The theocentric conception cannot be separated from anthropological self-understanding.

It is significant that Cohen tries to find a link between the position of God and that of human being by introducing the notion of revelation into the scope of a philosophical interpretation of faith or religion. Revelation, traditionally speaking, is related to human being, but it addresses human being in terms of specific contents, norms, commandments, and so forth. To be sure, revelation in that substantive meaning presupposes the human being's potentiality, accepting the contents of revelation. Revelation in this sense is addressed to the human being as a responsive being. Cohen probably does not deny the responding component of the human being's relation to revelation, but his main emphasis is on the human being's capacity as a reasonable being. Hence, revelation is not related to a special content but is a continuation of creation as the creation of human being. In revelation, the particular problem of human reason is emphasized. God does not reveal himself in something but in relation to something. Here again, revelation is a precondition and not a content (p. 82; p. 101), nor a spiritual event (p. 88; p. 109). Perhaps we have to understand spirituality as a background and not as a content. In a sense, Cohen tried to distinguish between revelation in its universal human sense and revelation as a historical event informing the biblical narrative, stressing that the human being, and not the people or even Moses, is the correlate of the God of revelation (p. 92; p. 117). The beginning should no longer be a beginning in time; it should connote an eternal origin (p. 98; p. 124).

* * *

These interpretations—and one could go on adding to them—point to the basic contention implied in the title of Cohen's major book on the issue: *Religion of Reason from the Sources of Judaism.* The textual or historical sources of the Hebrew Scripture are a kind of preparation for reason, that is, for the religion of reason. They are a kind of *praeparatio biblica.* The biblical text can be understood as alerting one to such issues as being, the ethical position of the individual human person, and even revelation as connoting the creation of man endowed with reason and not primarily as conveying commandments or norms to man. If we interpret religion or faith in its basic—that is, in the transhistorical sense—religion may become obsolete once we reach the level of reason referring both to being and to the manifestation of it in creation, including revelation. Concepts current in a philosophical system may be employed as means for the articulation of some dim elements present in the awareness of faith. But, in this conception, the inherent notions of faith become obsolete, or may become so, once we apply concepts grounded in a system to them. One can say that these concepts do not serve the purpose of reducing faith to that which is articulated through them. They serve rather the purpose of elevating that which is present but concealed in faith. Yet the possibility that faith will not be saved by that elevation inheres in Cohen's very interpretation of religion with the concepts of a religion of reason. We have here a systematic problem of a different order: is a philosophical interpretation or exposition meant to read conceptually that which is implicit in faith, or is it intended to transpose faith to a level differing fundamentally from it, claiming nonetheless to maintain an affinity between its textual expression and its philosophical articulation and justification? The aspect of justification seems to imply here the leveling of faith to the sphere of philosophy in the systematic sense.

There is indeed a difference between attempting to place faith within the sphere of feeling, which may prevent its coherent articulation, and the sphere of philosophy, which by definition is an activity of articulation. Yet perhaps that which Cohen presents is "overdone," philosophically speaking, since in the end it considers faith as a temporary phenomenon and not as a phenomenon in its own right. To be sure, there is a difference between criticizing the phenomenon of faith as being, for instance, obscure or primitive and elevating it to the sphere of a philosophical system. Yet we cannot but be aware of the trend of letting faith become immersed in a conceptual context that as such is not essentially one of faith. It is possible that an attempt to articulate faith without reducing or elevating it is a doomed enterprise because it cannot do justice to the variety of elements inherent in faith. Still, one should certainly be aware of the limits of articulation without pretending to present an adequate articulation. These problems will recur in the present analysis time and again and most expressly, as we shall see, in Hegel.

Thus far in this exposition we have encountered the ontological aspect of faith related to being in its purity. Faith is characterized not only by attitudes but also by specific assumptions about its correlate, God. As we proceed, we shall also have to consider some of these assumptions.

The critical consequence of my argument that faith cannot be subsumed by other categories and phenomena sets the direction of this study. It is meant to reinforce the view that faith and its various expressions is sui generis attitude. This thesis will therefore be dealt with from different points of view. The critical result leads next to an attempt to characterize faith in its own scope without placing it in the context of categories and phenomena that overshadow its specificity.

CHAPTER FOUR

Characterizations

We have thus far examined some philosophical expositions of the essence of faith. Our critique of these expositions focused on the common denominators of the varieties of faith. We noted the main thrust of these expositions has been to identify the essence of faith by identifying it with an attitude that by definition cannot be characteristic of faith alone. Structurally it does not matter whether the common denominator is feeling or reason since both factors or faculties are characteristic not only of faith. Feeling, of course, is a basic attitude or response, and reason underlies science and philosophy. Hence, we are obliged to wonder whether characterization of the specificity of faith is possible at all. Our skepticism is enhanced by the fact that historically faith was shaped in and by religions, that is, by a plurality of formulations. Accordingly, we are challenged to abstract from historical phenomena, as religions are, the essence of faith untainted by any historical interpretation.

We could thus proceed by arguing that we face an analogous problem with respect to art or science. In these spheres we may take a historical position and speak, for instance, about Greek tragedy or the modern novel. We may refer to geocentric astronomy and to heliocentric astronomy, indicating either the changes that occurred in the world conception or the fact that one direction of science has been superseded by another one. Still, the question of essence remains. Since faith takes the concrete shape of historical religions, the issue of historicity as well as of plurality may be of guiding significance. We face that issue constantly, and only a detailed examination of the phenomenon of faith will entitle us—if at all—to assert a tentative answer to that central question which is both methodological and systematic. With this issue in mind, I embark on the next step of my analysis. Positing a common denominator leads by definition to establishing the proximity between the phenomenon at stake and a factor outside it.

★   ★   ★

We now move to what can be considered a correlated aspect of faith, namely its object, though we should be aware that the term "object"—in this context only—has the meaning of a position and not of the inherent essence. This is because that to which faith refers cannot be just an object, a term originally connoting that which is vis-à-vis, as in the Greek *hypostasis*, that which underlies, or *Gegenstand* in German.

The Ontological Position

The Hebrew Scriptures contain some sporadic statements implying a conceptual rendering of the ontological position of the divine entity referred to in faith. One of the instances would be the name of *Yehovah* or *Yahweh*, which according to some interpretations contains the root *havoh*, "to be." Thus, the implied reference to the concept of being is already inherent in this name of God, and the implication becomes even more striking in the statement "I am that I am" (Exodus 3:14), which in Hebrew, using the root of "to be" in the future tense, points to the perpetual reality of God. An additional aspect should be mentioned, namely, "the glory of Israel will not lie" (Samuel 15:29) or, as it is sometimes translated, "the strength of Israel," though the root of the Hebrew for "glory" and "strength," *nezach*, implies the relation to eternity. In addition, the emphasis put on "not lying" is already an indication of the relation between the position of God in terms of his being and his behavior or attitude toward human beings. I mention these verses in order to indicate that perhaps conceptual articulations are not totally alien to the inherent essence of faith expressed in the basic text of biblical faith insofar as the ontological position of God is concerned. This does not imply that there is a continuity between the aspects of faith present in the Scriptures and those emphasized in philosophical interpretations.

The first aspect of biblical faith to be stressed is the extramundane position of the divine entity. That position does not imply the negation of mundane reality, which can be, and has been, one of the interpretations of the being of the divine entity. There may be coexistence between the mundane reality and the extramundane one. To be sure, in this case the difference in the ontological status of the two realities becomes prominent. However, the first emphasis is on the position of the divine entity as beyond or above the reality to which human beings belong.

The transcendence of the ontological status of divine reality leads to some primary conclusions, namely, that the divine reality cannot be seen or sensually perceived. To entertain faith is to take an attitude that differs from perception and even from cognition since its object is beyond the sphere of the usual modes of the awareness of objects. The mundane sphere may, of course, be a visible manifestation of the divine and thus can be considered a "theophany." The visibility of divine manifestations, however, does not allow one to assert that God himself is visible in his mundane manifestations. There are some consequences of this characterization of the ontological position of God as beyond the world: several names can be employed in our statements about the reality of God if we attempt to describe—or even to identify—that reality. The extramundane status may even lead to the conclusion that God is without name, since names, to some extent, imply an identification. But to identify God is impossible, for he is beyond all human categories. Hence, the extramundane divinity is not only without names but his transcendence also makes any expression about him impossible. Hence, God is called "ineffable"—as Cusanus put it. The divine reality is greater than anything that can be known or conceived. It need not be emphasized that the introduction of the concept of sublimity into this context is to some extent one of the consequences of the ineffable transcendence of the divine entity, whereby sublimity already evokes some attitude in the positive sense and is not confined to the negative characteriza-tions implied by the prefix "extra."

From the transcendence of the ontological position of the di-vine we may come to the concept of the absolute since "absolute" etymologically connotes that which is "separated from," or "ab-solved from" other entities. We cannot limit ourselves to the pri-mary etymological meaning, since "absolute" has the additional connotations of something standing by itself, being self-contained or self-sufficient, and thus may lead, and actually has led, to fur-ther characterizations of the divine as elevated and self-contained and thus perfect, as we shall see later. The distance from the mun-dane order inherent in the position of the divine as an extramun-dane entity with all its associated aspects often induces humans to assume an attitude of humility.

Yet when we consider humility as a component of faith, we ob-serve that we are not dealing only with the correlate of the lack of perception or knowledge but also with some consequences related to the human attitude or awareness. As Kant said, the sublime moves us and thus there is, as it were, a built-in response to the sub-lime, through which we refer to the implication of sublimity in terms of the qualities mentioned above. At this juncture, we shall recall a term or concept used in the Middle Ages, that of *aseitas*, which is seen as characteristic of the creator and as such opposed to mere existing, or *esse*. When this term was introduced, the con-text seemed to be not only the separated position of the divine en-tity but its characteristic self-contained essence as well. It is an entity enclosed in itself, though as a creator it is open to the world by the very act of establishing it. The reasoning behind this double aspect of self-enclosure and moving to the world seems to be grounded in the presupposed relation between *aseitas*, which is characteristic of reality, and the particular act inherent in the cre-ation of the world. The act is only an expression or a manifestation and not a motion, taking the self-enclosed entity out of its funda-mental essence as an actuality only. Therefore, any act directed to something outside the entity, like the world, does not introduce any change in the essence of that self-contained reality. On the contrary, since the act of creation is grounded in the ontological position of God, it reemphasizes the fact that the divine entity is without any origin; it is not created. Thus, while the notion of positing the world is not exposed to any change, the extramundane character of the divine entity does not lead us to discern any change or even motion within that entity.

* * *

The various aspects of going beyond perception or cognition have been summed up to some extent through the introduction of the term "transcending" or "transcendence," which has become rather characteristic of the discussions related to our subject matter. It is probably true to say that the verb "to transcend" terminologically preceded the substantive "transcendence." It can be said that the employment of the variations of the root "transcending" in religious vocabulary goes beyond what was described by Kant as something in general, or as an x, or negatively as that which is not an object of our sensuous intuition.

Transcendence is an equivalent of extramundanity. It is held to be a positive description of the divine position in the ontological sense of that term, though various expressions of the attitude of faith are aware of human limitations. These attitudes are nevertheless concerned with transcendence in the positive sense. One may refer to Kierkegaard and his remark that the individual stands in an absolute relation to the absolute. Knowledge is not implied in that statement, but the relation to the absolute is there as well as the position of the individual who is irreducible and maintains an absolute relation to the absolute correlate. We could add that the individual is aware of the absolute difference between himself and the absolute, and the relation as such exists with all these complexities. The distinction between perception and thinking is significant for the discernment of the background to the introduction of the notion of transcendence. One should recall Plato's view about being beyond being[1] and the continuation of that conception in Neoplatonism, where we already find an indication of

1. Plato, *Republic.*

bringing together the position and its content, which became prominent in the ensuing incorporation of the concept of transcendence into the attitude of faith. Transcendence makes possible the identification of divinity with the Holy Other and Otherness. A recurring statement that God is transcendent and unlimited perfection sums up to some extent the integration of the different aspects of God's ontological position with its essence inherent in the concept of perfection. Since we emphasize here the concept of transcendence as capturing the basic ontological direction of faith, a comment on the decidedly nontheistic faith of Buddhism and the notion of Nirvana might be appropriate.

In terms of the position of transcendence, Nirvana advocated by Buddhism occupies a particular and even a singular position. It does not only differ qualitatively from "mundane reality" or from any particular element contained in it. It is the other side of the nonreality of the mundane sphere. It is, one could say, the negative or negating telos of the mundane realm. That realm aims at or is driven to arrive at its own extinction; Nirvana implies that that process of extinction does eventually reach its goal. The unreality of the given world is to be fulfilled by extinction, and thus it is not just judged by the observer as nonreality but is realized in the transcendence denying its existence. Nonreality is to become a state of affairs by going beyond itself whether or not it is conscious of its position. Hence, transcendence is prominent in that conception of Nirvana; it is not only juxtaposed to a dependent reality, but it is also opposed to what is only seemingly a reality. To put it differently, paradoxical as it may sound: nonreality is to be realized de facto and as such is to be overcome not by way of intervention from the outside but by being prompted by its own inherent process. The dependence of the mundane on transcendence is replaced by the negation of the mundane, not through affirming transcendence but by pointing to its position as annihilating the mundane realm. This is not an act of transcendent reality, but its position as such brings about its impact on the mundane realm.

If the immersion in Nirvana were to be interpreted as ecstasy, here ecstasy would connote extinction or annihilation and not unification. In several interpretations in medieval philosophy, ecstasy connotes alienation or *alloisis* and not annihilation. It is related to *cognitio dei experementalis* or to *unio mystica*. As *unio,* it is a merging and not an extinction. Ecstasy is the act of moving out from the human position to the transcendent being. As a human act or attempt, it is bound to be sporadic, even when it is assumed that it reaches or may reach its goal. Implied in ecstasy is the difference between terrestrial reality and the transcendent one; the bridge is to establish a supercognitive act that as such is not set up on the level of reality. If successful, it leads to immersion in divine reality and not to the establishment of a level of reality. Apparently, the act of ecstasy as immersion does not annihilate those engaged in it. From this point of view, ecstasy in Buddhism differs from ecstasy as it has been interpreted in the various mystic trends in monotheistic religions.

Even if we do not accept Whitehead's conception of world loyalty as being *too* harmonious, we may say that faith inherently contains the awareness of human beings as belonging to the broader context of reality, beyond the interhuman or even terrestrial reality. Indeed, one of the possible interpretations of that belonging—and this is an interpretation and not a feeling—is that human beings are involved in what is beyond them—that is to say, they are related to transcendence, which because of its very position and essence posits the immanent. Various philosophical conceptions have tried to articulate this primary position of transcendence by different arguments and renderings. The point is to discern the hard core inherent at least in some of faith's manifestations. This "hard core" of faith, I shall argue, is the notion of creation.

The Impact of Transcendence

The presupposition that transcendence posits immanence is but the obverse side of the view that transcendence is superior to the mundane realm. That superiority is not of a static or architectonic character only but is manifested in transcendence's intervention in the whole scope of reality. Transcendence is understood as being capable of going beyond itself or, to put it topographically, below itself, while the mundane realm is destined to remain within its own boundaries and is incapable of overstepping them. Hence, power is said to be an essential attribute of transcendence. Power is the dynamic manifestation of the ontological status of transcendence. The relation or affinity between the attitude of faith and the concern with the active impact of transcendence on the immanent realm is expressed in the notion of creation.

The distinction between the terrestrial as given and the transcendent does not necessarily lead to an interpretation of the relation between the two realms that assigns superiority to the latter. Let us mention Kant's distinction between sense-data and the thing-in-itself, which to a very large extent is a distinction based on architectonic considerations and does not imply the active position of the thing-in-itself in relation to sensuous data. In contrast, religious faith in its various expressions assumes an active relation between the mundane order and the transcendent realm, in which the latter also takes the initiative. This presupposition of faith probably has several motivating factors, even beyond a possible cognitive or supracognitive one. The search for relationships between the two realms goes beyond mere description. It is an attempt to identify something that is not comprehended in the static presence of the respective realms. The aspect of relation between the spheres may be considered an attempt at surmising—and here we come back to the relation between conjecture and faith—that which goes beyond visual and rational discernment or identification.

One can point to two aspects of facing something that is mysterious. The first is the very facticity of the reality we encounter as human beings, that is, our own reality or existence or the broad scope of reality that we experience or to which we address ourselves by extrapolating what we experience. The relations that we are looking for are not those within the sphere of reality but in a realm outside that sphere. Thus, the mysterious character of facticity is integrated into our experience as implying a relation to the mysterious character of transcendence. One mysterious fact is paradoxically explained by another, and the two are epitomized in the mysterious relation between them. Conjecture may go beyond the identification of levels toward looking for a contact between the identified different realms of reality. Knowledge, exemplifying the cognitive attitude, is by and large concerned—or in the present context, we may say confined—to the identification of objects and the relations between them. What of the universe of objects? Is it related at all or just present? And if it is related, to what? Faith comes into this context if we try to identify its direction and raison d'être. Faith is not knowledge. It is an awareness; it contains elements of knowledge but goes beyond them and attempts to explain by way of addressing itself to the inexplicable and by offering an explanation that is a nonexplanation.

The inexplicable character of the facticity of mundade reality, as already noted, is faith's point of departure. Faith is not confined to pointing to the inexplicability of facts, but attempts to go beyond them, even when that step beyond is only a conjecture. Indeed, one can always question the conjecture and, in this sense, one could ask how it is that there is transcendence at all. But the continuous or even circular character of conjecture does not cancel that which prompts faith. In this respect, faith may be considered an escape from reasoning; indeed, it is the very nature of faith to escape the bonds of reason, or to use a paradoxical expression, it is its raison d'être.

⋆ ⋆ ⋆

Some topics widely discussed in classical philosophical discourse, such as whether creation is out of nothingness, are to a very large extent of secondary significance in terms of our major subject. The issue of a material background preceding creation raises the question of the facticity of that background: the component of mystery returns even when creation is to some extent limited by the presence of that facticity. The point is that creation is an activity to be located between the creator and nothingness, and nothingness refers here not to that which preceded or did not precede the act of creation but to the world that would not exist or be present without the activity of creation.

The major juxtaposition is between the nothingness of the world and its reality. Faith starts from the assumption, articulated or not, that the presence of the world is not explainable within the boundaries of the world as such. That presence calls for an intervention stemming from transcendence that is a reality beyond the world and, to use a geometrical metaphor, above it. Other philosophical discussions as to the presence of the transcendent within the world once the immanent realm has been posited are also of secondary significance because the positing—or "creating"—of the world can leave the world to itself (the deistic argument), but it can also lead to the assumption that the activity of positing, once exhibited, is not limited or exhausted in the initial act (the position of theistic religions). As we shall see, the continuous impact of transcendence on the immanent, mundane order may be understood, as in Spinoza's system, as the elision of the transcendent. From the point of view of faith, the relation of transcendence and immanence is highlighted with the notions of revelation and providence, and these have to be discussed in some detail.

⋆ ⋆ ⋆

Architectonically speaking, at this juncture, I must already point to two directions in the relation between creation and that which is created. One direction inherent in the very notion of creation, of course, is that from transcendence to immanence; the other is from immanence to transcendence. Religion, taken in the sense of an articulation of faith, is concerned with both directions. Though we may say that, while faith may also contain the direction from human beings to the facticity of transcendence, religion, being at least a more formulated attitude or awareness, is more concerned with both directions together. This observation will repeatedly recur in my analysis.

The relation between mundane reality and the realm of transcendence is two-sided: mundane reality is understood as dependent on its being posited ("created") by the realm of transcendence. The realm of transcendence, by positing the realm of mundane reality, is directed toward it. Divine positing on the one hand and human dependence on the other are interpreted as creation. This interpretation attributes to dependence a reference of a specific character expressed in the divine act of creation. The superior position of transcendence becomes manifest in that reference to the immanent realm. The two-sided relation does not obscure the superiority of the transcendent realm. This interpretation is valid not only in the context of monotheistic religions but also in paganism, for the deity in pagan religions is present in the world in spite of the plurality of deities, even if the deity is not understood as becoming manifest in an act of "creation."

Transcendence is understood as being independent of immanent reality. Thus it is given, or, to put it differently, it is preexistent. In this sense, philosophical articulations of transcendence have to a very large extent taken the direction of emphasizing the aspect of *causa sui*. In addition, transcendence has been understood both as a realm and as an entity, and the leap—to use that term again—to God as transcendent is grounded in the conjunction between these aspects of transcendence as being both a separate realm and that of an entity. Nevertheless, faith comes to the fore precisely when human beings, who are part of the immanent order, make reference to the transcendent one. Transcendence becomes significant within the horizon of human interpretation of that which is given to human beings through their intentionality toward that which is beyond the given: the transcendent reality is beyond that which is given or present within the scope of mundane human experience.

Again, as we have seen from several perspectives, faith is an interpretation and not an experience. Faith points not to an object encountered but to an object viewed—or interpreted—as amplifying that which we encounter in a piecemeal way in our meeting with that which is given. In addition, although the transcendent realm is interpreted as positing mundane reality, we cannot intentionally reach that realm unless we interpret the immanent reality—negatively—as fundamentally lacking self-sufficiency. Suppose that immanent reality were self-supporting or self-sufficient, then the step taken toward the transcendent realm would be not a leap but a kind of hypothesis for its own sake. Moreover, the conjunction between transcendence as a realm and an entity, which is a basic feature of some religions, is again an interpretation and as such it informs the notion of creation. Creation is understood as establishing mundane reality by way of the action or intervention of a cause that is beyond that reality. That cause is not necessarily to be interpreted as a personal, intentional act. But when the transcendent cause is understood as that of a creator, we introduce a personal agent (qua transcendent entity) into the scope of these deliberations. The act of creation is thus grounded in the essence of the creator as a transcendent entity.

At this juncture we encounter some significant features of faith as interpretation. The conjunction between transcendence and cause already brings something that we meet within the immanent realm into the scope of the interpretation: one event depends on another, and regularly on the preceding one. The aspect of precedence is interpreted by faith as an aspect of preexistence. This again is an interpretation grounded in human experience or awareness but expanded in the direction of the relation between the mundane and the transcendent. Nevertheless, we find the interpretation of the activity of the transcendent realm as creation grounded in the creator and again expressing him as an expansion of human experience, that is, of the sphere of human relations where a given act or action is experienced as a manifestation of a given agent. Though the realm of transcendence is beyond the sphere of human experience, we thus notice that faith is not satisfied with outlining topologically, as it were, the various realms.

By pointing to relations between the spheres, faith bases itself on some structural elements of the human experience. In this sense, we may conclude that faith takes over the anthropomorphic structure of experience and transposes it to the realm that by definition is beyond experience. The fact that I am employing the loaded term "anthropomorphic" does not imply critical reservation as when I refer to anthropomorphic expressions used in attributing certain qualities, such as mercy, to the pure divine entity. In the anthropomorphic direction, we find an assessment of the basic fact that faith is an attitude or intentionality, as it has been traditionally described, *a parte homini.* Faith referring to God is not an expression *a parte Dei.* One of the possible expressions of this paradoxical double-sided relation between the immanent sphere and the transcendent realm is expressed in the view that without God we are unable to know God.

★ ★ ★

At this point, one may comment on the position of transcendence in some twentieth-century philosophical trends. First, Heidegger says that being is always the being of a specifically existent being (*eines Seiendes*). He calls this level of being "ontic" and contrasts it with the "ontological" or the fundamental conditions of possibility or structure of the totality of that which is. This totality in turn marks the phenomenological horizon of the ontic, and so Heidegger refers to it as transcendent. As such, however, transcendence remains tied to the immanence of reality. Hence Heidegger speaks of being as *transcendens schlechthin*[2]—a term to which I shall refer later and seek to analyze further. Here it will suffice to note that transcendence as ontological in Heidegger's sense cannot be an object of human intentionalitiy and therefore does not posit faith. Faith, in contrast, is grounded in a human intentionality understanding itself as lacking self-sufficiency. We shall return time and again to this double-faceted or paradoxical position of faith.

Thus I come to the conclusion that with respect to faith the notion of horizon cannot be an adequate translation of transcendence. This conclusion is reinforced when we consider Jaspers's notion of philosophical faith, which is grounded in the self-transcendence of human existence.[3] Self-transcending—that is, what goes outside, beyond, or above human existence—retains human existence within the realm of immanence. The act of self-transcendence takes place within the realm of immanence; going beyond the limitations of human existence does not imply intentionality toward transcendence, let alone the affirmation of a permanent mutual relation between the spheres. To be sure, we can

2. Heidegger, *Sein und Zeit*, par. 69 ff.

3. This is the theme of Karl Jaspers, *Der philosophische Glaube*. Also consult Karl Jaspers, *Philosophy of Existence*, trans. with an introduction by Richard F. Graban (Philadelphia: University of Pennsylvania Press, 1971), pp. 63 ff.

argue phenomenologically that faith is one of the expressions or manifestations of self-transcendence as a phenomenon of human existence or intentionality. It might be interpreted as the *genus proximum* of the intentionality of faith. However, self-transcendence is not faith and cannot be understood as grounding faith in the philosophical sense if we wish to remain true to the inherent and essential quality of faith. Unlike "philosophical faith," which has a dynamic processual character, faith in the authentic sense of the term not only reaches out but "comes" to the realm of transcendence via being aware of the distance between itself and that realm. This is seen more strikingly in the variations on the notion of mystical union that are applied to the union between man and God. Hence, we can say, trying to shed light on the essence of faith, that a mystical union can be understood as the ultimate manifestation of faith but that it is impossible within the orbit of philosophical faith. The mystical union is, indeed, a union and not an ongoing process of self-transcendence. Self-transcendence may be understood as the background of the union, but the latter clearly goes beyond the limits of that process.

The particular position of humans within the scope of their relation to transcendence is—and this may sound trivial—inherent in faith as such. The position of humans within faith is highlighted by that act of the divine entity directed toward humans that is traditionally called revelation.[4]

⋆   ⋆   ⋆

Our awareness of what surrounds us is at its core—the awareness of facticity. We do not encounter the factual world as a whole; what we encounter, we expand to its limits by speaking about immanent reality or facticity. The point of departure of faith seems to be the attempt to conjecture a positive correlate to the primary negative assertion, namely, that immanent reality cannot be self-contained. Because of that assertion, faith moves or leaps to two

4. Heidegger, *Sein und Zeit*, par. 53 ff.

assertions: the first assertion is the reality of the transcendent realm, and the second is that that realm contains in itself the explanation for the facticity of the immanent realm.[5]

The first assertion is an assertion proper, though there is no evidence for it, in the cognitive sense of the term. Hence, it can be fertile ground for the affirmation in faith of transcendence. The second step is more of a conjecture because it assumes the significance of the transcendent realm for the immanent one by the fact or act that transcendence posits the immanent. Here we have to observe that these two moves toward transcendence can be interpreted as "borrowing" for the sake of faith from religion, in both its historical and the structural sense. The borrowing is expressed in interpreting transcendence as the realm out of which creation takes place and even more so by assuming the relation between creation and creator. The reliance on religion in this context is due to several aspects of the basic relation between faith and religion. We shall return to that issue.

At this juncture, we may say that faith—in presenting an attitude of reliance on transcendence—may take advantage of some articulations inherent in religions; one of these is the concept of creation and creator. Faith finds its refuge in these concepts because they affirm a relationship between realms that cannot be considered as warranted by the usual procedures of the cognitive attitude. Faith brings together the awareness of facticity in its own boundaries and in pointing to the realm beyond or above itself. Faith here evokes a conviction but concurrently also, at least potentially, a skeptical nuance as to the validity of that conviction.

This aspect of faith can be emphasized by a comparison between what is considered a scientific explanation of the existence of the world and the explanation inherent in faith. Scientific discourse may offer statements such as this: one possible answer is to say that God chose the initial configuration of the universe for reasons that we cannot hope to understand. The very use of the phrase

5. Emanuel Levinas formulated his conception in his different writings. I refer here to his book *Totality and Infinity* (1961) and to some of his articles included in *The Levinas Reader*, ed. Sean Hand (Oxford: Blackwell, 1989), pp. 49 ff., and in *God and Philosophy*, pp. 166 ff.

"reasons that we cannot hope to understand" has the nuance of faith since it asserts that something is being stated that we cannot possibly comprehend. Yet when it is said, "There may be a large number of models of the universe with different initial conditions that all obey laws," then we see that the reference to laws is an indication that the explanation must be related to a structure of laws, and these in turn connote the order between events, and not the order between events and something outside them. If it is said that there ought to be some principle that picks out one initial state, then again, it is assumed that the origin is related to a principle and not to a realm and a particular act attributed to it. The cosmological attempts do not isolate these endeavors from the basic scientific approach even when they use some, as it were, linguistic associations suggesting the texture of expressions characteristic of faith. In addition, the attitude of faith refers to a realm and not to an initial link in a chain of deductions, principles, and so on. The transcendent realm is affirmed not by reference to principles but by the direction of faith proper.

Being aware of the transposition of concepts present in religions—to faith in its basic or initial character—we must point out a certain limit to that transposition. Many religious manifestations are not satisfied with grounding creation in the creator but offer some explanation for the fact that creation occurred, and those explanations are considered in turn to be grounded in the essence of the creator. A significant expression of that explanation or quasi-explanation is the describing or identifying of the essence of the creator as goodness. As such, the world is understood as expressing the *bonum,* or the goodness, of the creator. Hence, not only is it assumed that creation inheres in the goodness of the creator, but also the attributes animating his act of creation with a motivation can be conceptually identified. Yet we have already seen that the step from creation to a creator is grounded in human experience, whereby a given situation is assumed to be an expression of an intended action of a particular agent.

At this point, one may come back to the philosophical interpretation of transcendence as formulated by Heidegger. In the first place Heidegger uses the term *transcendens,* saying that being is the *transcendens* in the strict sense of the term *schlechthin*. The adverb *schlechthin* recalls its use by Schleiermacher in characterizing faith as the feeling of dependence *schlechthin*. Yet, it is probably not an accident that Heidegger uses the term *transcendens* in the form of a participle and not in the form of a substantive, thus possibly indicating that the reference here is to the process and not to the realm. Immediately after this formulation, he comes back to the substantive *Transendenz* of the being of the existent and combines the two with the term "transcendental," concluding the statement with the conjunction *veritas transcendentalis*. It is again not by chance that, in this context, the reference is to phenomenological truth that amounts to the openness of being.

The difference between "transcendence" and *transcendens*—to reiterate this point—must be considered as a basic one. Transcendence is a realm and as such is not encountered and cannot be considered as being open. The act of creation makes it present and effective, but not open, while the participle *transcendens* may point to a process and its results, which we encounter in our immanent experience. The "I" is more than what one experiences here and now, and thus we transcend the present moment by assuming an identity transcending it. The language we speak is a context beyond our own presence. We draw from its reservoir by actualizing it in our speaking. Our fellow human beings transcend the boundaries of our own existence. We identify them as persons, thus establishing or implying a relation between their presence and human essence. The institutions in which we dwell or operate transcend our own scope. Hence, we arrive at the conclusion that the process of transcending is part of our experience, precisely because experience is not limited to the instantaneous. However, all this does not offer the ground for the affirmation of the realm of transcendence that is both conceptually primary to our concern and essential for what is intentionally referred to in faith.

The step taken from facticity to transcendence occurs at the other end of the realm of reality. It is not related to the position of human beings, though human beings are tacitly present as interpreters of the step taken. There is an additional aspect of faith, again not unrelated to religions, that focuses on human beings, namely revelation. My next concern will thus be with revelation as a manifestation of transcendence addressed to human beings, either as individuals or as a collective.

One additional comment might be appropriate here. The horizon of experience is not the transcendent reality. It is the comprehensive framework of all that is given. That which is given relates to the horizon of experience, but the horizon does not relate to transcendence and thus cannot be interpreted as creating it. Philosophical self-transcendence, as we have seen, is an ongoing process, but it does not affirm the reality beyond the process. It is in a sense an existential transformation of the "asymptotic character" of knowledge as conceived by the neo-Kantians. As a process it cannot be seen as self-contained but, rather, as an extrapolation of experience. Because of this consideration we may ask, Why should we employ the notion of faith in this context altogether since there is no relation to reality beyond experience?

CHAPTER FIVE

Manifested Guidance

Let me reiterate that introducing the notion of creation into the context of articulating various components of faith is an act of "borrowing" from articulated religions. Yet there are different levels or modes of "borrowing." I take an example from the widespread interpretation of creation as related to the prime cause or that which is dependent on it. Culturally and texturally this interpretation is obviously a transposition of a formulated philosophical concept to the texture of religious expressions. The biblical texts speak of the act or event of creation, but we should not ground it in a cause in the systematic sense of that term. The situation is different with regard to the proximity between faith and the religious notion of creation since several presuppositions implicit in the attitude of faith lead to the notion of creation, even when we consider the move to that notion a sort of terminological leap and obviously not a logical necessity.

It is therefore appropriate to consider some aspects of the affinity between faith and the notion of creation. In the first place, it should be emphasized that the introduction of the notion of creation is already an interpretation of factual reality one encounters, and it presupposes awareness of factual reality on the part of the interpreters, as well as an awareness of an additional feature of that reality, namely, that it cannot be self-contained.

In this sense, faith is a form of exploration of reality, assuming that an exploration of the sort suggested by it is bound to refer to something beyond factual reality. Whether creation is to be interpreted as an act or as a continuous presence of that which is within reality but beyond the multiplicity of the parts of that reality—as we find in the Upanishads—is already an additional step in the interpretation of creation. Because the presence of transcendence within immanence blurs the distinction between the two, that presence is additionally expressed in the identification of the essence of human being with transcendence as understood in the notion of *Isvara*. The least that can be said in terms of the reference to the notion of creation is that reality encountered evokes the awareness—and thus the interpretation—that there is something outside or beyond it; that which is outside and beyond has an effect on turning reality into facticity and thus making it present.

⋆   ⋆   ⋆

A second step can again be characterized by borrowing yet another notion from religions. This is the notion of revelation. To be sure, there are some interpretations of facticity as dependent on creation as revelation, that is to say, creation is already a revelation of transcendent reality or the divine agent. Yet it seems more appropriate to deal with the notion of revelation in the context of human reality and not in that of comprehensive factual reality. To be sure, human awareness and interpretation lead to placing human existence within factual reality. Human beings are aware of the primary fact that they do not bring themselves about, and thus they find themselves, insofar as awareness goes, as factually given or present. But that factual aspect does not exhaust human awareness because of the additional ingredient present within the basic human horizon, namely what human beings must do once they are aware of the encompassing reality. I refer, for instance, to John 1:10: "He was in the world, and the world was made by him, and the world knew him not." What is implied here is the hidden or tacit presence of the creator, a presence that as such does not lead immediately, or let us say, automatically, to awareness or knowledge of the relation between the world and him who made it. Hence, an additional step relating to the word is implied in John, namely, "and the word was made flesh." What is significant here is the transition not from the word and hearing or receiving it, but to the flesh, that is, to incarnation. Still, a special relationship is emphasized in this context between the word and the orbit of human reality. Thus, we can consider a further step in the direction of manifestation: the step toward human beings as verbally or conceptually addressed. This position presupposes a relation between Logos and human beings as endowed with the capacity of receiving the Logos.

⋆   ⋆   ⋆

Revelation has essentially two meanings or directions. Human beings receive the divine word, and they are endowed with the capacity of receiving it. The very capacity of human beings to receive revelation presupposes their ability, at least to some extent, to comprehend it. Revelation thus underscores the facticity of human beings as denizens of the mundane order who through faith seek to go beyond it. The content of revelation provides guidance, mainly in the normative sense, to attain a relationship with transcendence.

The act of endowing human beings with a special capacity and the focusing of the content of revelation on norms may be regarded as a continuation of the primary act of creation. These nuances in the relation between creation and revelation are evident in the various interpretations of revelation as presenting the name of the creator to human beings, as well as his power and sublimity as manifest in his very intention to guide them.

The interconnectedness of creation and revelation is further seen when creation is considered as an intervention of the transcendent reality in the immanent one, and revelation is understood as divine intervention within the specific human context. Hence, at least in some of the religious conceptions, revelation has been interpreted as a divine manifestation within the context of history. Berkeley has formulated this philosophically: transcendence is different in kind, more excellent in degree than what lies open to the common sense of man.[1] Because of that difference,

1. George Berkeley, *The Sixth Dialogue of Alciphron, or the Minute Philosopher* (1732) in *Works*, ed. T. E. Jessup (London: Thomas Nelson & Sons, 1950), 3:240.

transcendence can intervene in the human reality and therefore, perhaps, respond to the human need or expectation to be guided since, without that guidance, human beings would be utterly immersed in their factual reality, lacking norms of conduct. Hence, it is appropriate to emphasize—in relation to the notion of revelation—not only the factual intervention but also the imperative or normative direction of that intervention. In the biblical text, we find a focused interpretation of that normative position in the assumption that human beings are created in the image of God and that their imitation of God is the supreme or basic norm of their conduct—formulated—and conveyed to them in revelation.

The question one should ask here is, In what sense can we consider revelation akin to faith? It could be said that, since faith is a conjecture, it is not totally ungrounded or without full foundation in some experienced aspects of reality. As such, faith relates to the conjecture that human beings are not left to themselves, that there is a response on the part of the creator or the revealing entity in the direction of guiding them. What was said above—that the receiver interprets himself as being endowed with the capacity of reception—can be seen as a corollary aspect of revelation.

In this sense, revelation can be considered as an opening and therefore as an enlightenment. I mention in this context that the meaning of Buddha is "enlightened"—that his achievement of awareness of the structure of the universe was an enlightenment. He arrived at it in the twenty-seventh year of his life; that is, the enlightenment was not innate in him but was the result of a process. Enlightenment here does not imply a historical event but a cognitive opening or uncovering. Hence, it can be understood why revelation has been interpreted as *theophania*. Here too, the disclosure of the divine entity may apply to revelation as well as to creation.

★   ★   ★

Remaining within the boundaries of faith proper, it is appropriate to remark on the relation between faith and confidence. This is so, not only because of the etymological affinity between the two words, but because faith—as accepting guidance—implies confidence that the guidance will be forthcoming or that there are grounds to expect a particular response from the revealing entity. Confidence is a persuasion, not a knowledge, and thus is close to faith. It is a disposition and not an erratic act. It motivates conduct because it refers to the normative component of revelation. Confidence is exposed to disappointment, and faith encounters the problem here of whether disappointment can undermine faith or whether some explanation is to be looked for through confidence in order to compensate for the disappointment. There is thus a proximity between revelation, confidence, and reliance, whereby reliance also presupposes some self-understanding of human beings of their relation to the revealing entity or realm. The aspect of expectation inherent in confidence leads one to emphasize the affinity between "believing in" and the relation between confidence and faith.

Having tried to bring out the affinity between faith and revelation, I refer to what can be understood as one of the cardinal aspects of faith. We should, however, distinguish between this aspect and some persistent interpretations of revelation that obviously go beyond its basic meaning. I refer to concepts like providence or predestination, which obviously imply dependence on a creator who not only reveals himself but constantly watches over human behavior as well. We can again discern some "logic" in the move from revelation to providence. But as long as we maintain the difference between the basic meaning of concepts and their inherence in faith, we must draw a demarcation line between faith and the more formulated concepts that are part of some religious attitudes but do not necessarily belong to the realm of faith as such. To be sure, the relation between faith and religion has to be seen as relevant for the whole topic before us, and so I shall try to address it.

Another basic concept lies on the borderline between faith and religion, namely, the concept of the divine entity or God. The question is, What are the possible considerations leading to the move or leap from the transcendent realm qua realm to the divine entity, that is, an entity with personal attributes. This will be our next topic.

CHAPTER SIX

Being

I have employed the term "borrowing" several times to indicate some conceptual rendering of the attitude of faith. If faith is an attitude, then in order to describe it, let alone identify it, we are obliged to "borrow" or to avail ourselves of a terminological or conceptual apparatus, that is by definition outside the genuine or basic essence of faith. Hence, the question preoccupying any exposition of this sort is whether the "borrowed" terms or concepts can be conceived as being truly akin to the essence of faith.

This consideration can be underlined by recalling our analysis of the basic assumption that factual reality is not self-contained or self-sufficient and, as such, points—or rather is interpreted as pointing—to the transcendent realm. Faith presupposes a distinction between factual reality and, if I may be allowed the term, real or intimate reality. The move to the latter cannot be demonstrated. Faith takes that move as expressing its attitude both in the direction of viewing factual reality as it is and of assuming its dependence on the transcendent, "higher" reality. In a sense, faith believes—supposes—that there is such a transcendent reality. When we refer to creation and revelation, it is clear that these occurrences are not factually given; they are assumed, or affirmed in conjecture. I used the description "acts" earlier; essentially, acts presuppose events, or acts are interpretations of events. Events are not given but are affirmed in faith, and, by virtue of faith, factual and real reality are linked.

* * *

These characterizations of the attitude of faith lead us to two systematic conclusions. Faith is an attitude referring to something beyond the scope of human experience, but it is nevertheless a human attitude or, in phenomenological terminology, an intentionality. The human perspective cannot be eliminated even when we take an extreme theocentric view. Transcendence is affirmed from the perspective of human experience and its encounter with factual reality. The second systematic point to be noted here is that faith, not to mention religion, interprets transcendent reality not only as present within the scope of intentionality but also as ultimate being; that is, an ontological position is attributed to what is, to use the phenomenological terminology, the noematic pole of intentionality or of noetic acts.

The interrelation between the two aspects of intentionality—noesis and noema—is inherent in the act of faith, but the ontological interpretation adds a dimension to the noematic pole. Hence, even if Van Der Leeuw's observation is warranted, namely, that God is a latecomer in the history of religion,[1] this fact does not belie the fact that the inherent thrust of faith—built into its phenomenological structure—points necessarily to the concept of God. In this sense, its conceptual expressions have to be considered as essential to faith, whatever the historical process of its formulations.

Terminologically, let us observe that the English term "being" has two connotations: a given reality and a specific entity. This coalescence of the two distinct meanings of the term differs from what we find, for instance, in Greek as the distinction between *ousia* and *on*, let alone in Hebrew between *havayah* and *Yahveh*, though the two are variations of the same root (see p. 41, above). I shall consider first some aspects of being in the sense of a given reality and, so to speak, ontological position, before I consider what are traditionally called "attributes" (of God), which refer to being as an entity rather than to being as a given reality.

* * *

1. G. Van der Leeuw, *Religion in Essence and Manifestation: A Study in Phenomenology*, trans. J. E. Turner (London: George Allen & Unwin, 1967), p. 48.

The first aspect to be considered in this context is that which in later medieval philosophy was called "the absolute." The absolute is basically that which is separated and, in this sense, may be conceived as congruous with the transcendent. Moreover, the medieval philosophers spoke also of the *absolutissima,* a term that emphasizes not only the separated level of being but also the totality of the separation or, negatively speaking, emphasizes that there is no way of obscuring the distinction between the separated, transcendent reality and the factual, mundane one. In fact, the concept of the absolute has been employed as one of the descriptions of the essence of God, but from a systematic view we can use this description as characteristic of transcendent reality as such. Because of the distinction between the factual and the real, the real is by definition different and thus separated from the factual. Hence, it is possible to interpret the real as synonymous with transcendence and consequently as absolute.

We now move from the concept of the absolute to the concept of incomprehensibility. If the transcendent is separated from the factual, it cannot be compared with it. Thus, in the light of this consideration, the transcendent is also called *absconditus.* In the attempt to discern certain aspects—in the concept of transcendence—that have been interpreted as attributes of God, we can employ the concept of incomprehensibility in relation to transcendence. Notice the comparative aspect of these descriptions with regard to both the concept of the absolute and that of incomprehensibility. That which is beyond the scope of human experience is sometimes characterized negatively as separated and beyond the reach of comprehension. The comparative point of departure leads to an antithetical statement: since the entity is beyond human scope, it is incomprehensible. In addition, we can say that these descriptions pointing to the ontological position of being also express the assumed value of transcendence precisely because what is placed as beyond human experience is understood as above—and thus higher than—that experience in terms of its possible and real impact on the realm of immanence. This transcendence is said to have the quality of the sublime.

In the Middle Ages, an additional term was sometimes brought into the context of these discussions, namely, being of an underived existence, God is understood as *aseitas,* sometimes rendered in English as "aseity." In employing this term, the emphasis was put on the ontological position of transcendence as being totally independent, not only incomparable in its status but also underivable. Thus, there is no affinity between transcendent reality and the immanent one, notwithstanding the possibility that transcendent reality has a fundamental impact on the immanent terrestrial order: creating it. The impact is not related to any proximity between the two realms; it is an expression of the superior position of the transcendent realm. Even if one entertains the view that there are levels within the transcendent realm—as, for instance, in Plato's concept of ideas and the idea of Good, from the angle of experience—the possible hierarchy within the realm of transcendence is not decisive with respect to its basic ontological position.

★   ★   ★

We are led to a fourth description of the transcendent, indeed, the most common one: the aspect of eternity. Eternity is conceived as an everlasting existence or as an ontological position or status that has no beginning and no end. Eternity, attributed to the transcendent entity, connotes that the entity will never cease to be real. As such, it is conceptually and ontologically different from factual reality, which is a sum total of transitory beings, past, present, and future. From the various discussions of the notion of eternity, we learn that eternity has sometimes been attributed to the world in the universal sense of the term but also to God as a transcendent reality. What has been stressed in terms of that reality is the everlasting presence of the eternal. In Greek philosophy, the metaphor used was that of fire, to emphasize that this is a self-regenerating reality. Whatever the interpretation of eternity, it has been conceived as one of the attributes of transcendent reality.

To summarize this part of the exposition, I have argued that the four aspects of transcendence I have discussed can be conceived as aspects of being in general or as marking transcendence as a separate, superior realm of being, and not of an entity interpreted as containing in itself these four aspects. Hence, the next step will be from being in general to being as understood as synonymous with God. Here we shall consider specific attributes, to employ the term frequently found used in medieval thought. We shall argue that there is a difference between the aspects relating to the position of transcendent being—or those related to the ontological status of transcendence—and the attributes characterizing the conduct and ways of God. It is not by chance that we differentiate between positional aspects and attributes, for attributes are more properly conceived as descriptions of God's actions.

In the previous analysis, I pointed to descriptions of transcendence that are meant to emphasize its self-enclosed character. As a matter of fact, the four descriptions I considered can be regarded as four variations on the same theme because they are all attempts to formulate the self-contained essence of transcendence. There is nothing beyond it from the perspective of facticity or of what we experience within the scope of immanent reality. In contrast, attributes are essentially characterizations of the divine entity not only conceived from the human point of view but also meant to present the actions of that entity as paradigmatic for human conduct. There is therefore a difference between interpretation of a *noema* and interpretation of its reference to human beings and their expected conduct. An additional consideration should be taken into account, namely, that there is a plurality of divine attributes which are not variations of the same theme but symbolize various guiding norms. Thus there is at least the possibility of a tension or even of a clash between the different attributes. This in turn has to be considered once we assume that transcendence is a realm in the positional ontological sense, whereas transcendence conceived as an entity may lead to an attempted synthesis of both aspects of transcendence, namely, as a separate—superior, sublime—realm and as a personal being.

CHAPTER SEVEN

Entity, Cognition, and Reality

Entity

I will now consider one of the turning points of the attitude of faith. Literally, we could say that the move from being in general to being as an entity is a step toward concentration, but it is not enough to dwell on this aspect. In the articulation of the different aspects of faith we may observe a central issue, namely, that being as an entity is endowed with predicates that are meant to express its essence. It is not enough that the entity cannot be separated from the essence since the ontological position of absoluteness can be seen as essence or belonging to essence. Predicates like spirituality or joy are beyond the articulation of essence qua position in the ontological sense. Indeed, we find predicates attributed to being even in what can be described as religions not centered around the concept of a personal God. Thus, for instance, Atman is viewed as the light and Brahman as an observer even when not conceived as active. In addition, Brahman is conceived in terms of unlimited power, and therefore the predicates in this case are those not only of being but also of spirituality and joy. Joy is possibly attributed to Brahman because it is considered congruous with self-containment or, to put it negatively, not dependent on another entity. Terminologically, we find the move from being in general to being as an entity expressed in words like *deitas*, which is considered as *essentia Dei*, or in the distinction between *deitas* and *divinitas*, and so forth.

Were we entitled to employ the notion of "reason for" in this context, we might be led to ask for the reason or reasons for introducing the distinction between being in general and being as an entity. The dependence of immanent reality as the sum total of facticity is dependent on something higher than itself and thus could probably be interpreted as implying a basic awareness of the dependence of facticity on transcendence. This awareness does not, of course, imply an encounter with fact. It is rather indicative of the attitude of faith and may lead to the conception that transcendence has a particular power vis-à-vis that which depends on it. Hence, as we have already noted, power or might are attributed to transcendence.

Yet the predicate of power or might seems not to exhaust the essence of transcendence, though the line of causality is emphasized in various trends of thought, leading from divine power to the affirmation of God as the ultimate cause of all occurrences and knowledge. What has been characterized as the "line" of negation could be considered as the other side of the "line" of causality, since the transcendent being is considered totally different from that which causally depends on it.

"Eminence" is conceived as related to the highest value of the highest good and as such does not refer by way of articulation only to the essence of the transcendent being. We find some interpretations understood as specifying the basic attribute of eternity, for instance, as being alive. Still, attributes like being able, wise, or willing are additional interpretations and cannot be conceived— though they are sometimes presented as such—as articulating the basic attribute of eternity. The oscillation characteristic of many trends of faith can be summed up by pointing to the fact that the transcendent is considered nameless because of its separated position but at the same time allowing or even calling for many different names, while these in turn manifest the hidden essence, expressed by way of attributes.

★ ★ ★

To be sure, the whole consideration of the essence of the transcendent being cannot be separated from the basic aspect of faith, though that aspect can be considered paradoxical. On the one hand, faith as an intentionality refers to that which is above human beings; yet on the other hand the characteristic features of human existence are brought into the direction of faith, for instance, knowledge. It is said that the Lord is the God of knowledge. In that sense, the attribute of knowledge is related to a dependence exhibited in the position of transcendence in relation to facticity or even in revelation as a divine disclosure of knowledge guiding human beings. The attribute of knowledge is present in human self-awareness and is possibly considered one of the most significant aspects of human existence. As such, it could not be viewed as present in a realm beyond human existence. If it is considered in this way, it is brought into the realm of transcendence from its presence within the scope of human experience.

By way of interpretation, it has been said that the attribute of knowledge as a quality of divine essence is symbolic in meaning because of the underlying comparison between the different realms of reality. In addition, when it is said that human acts of knowledge imply the difference between the act and the object to which they refer, whereas in the divine realm the act and the object coincide, we see again the comparative aspect of the attribution of knowledge to God. The distinction between the act—though going beyond what is essential in the human sphere—and the object is derived from the human realm and is taken to be overcome in the divine realm while still referring to that which is overcome, namely, the characteristic qualities of the human realm. Interpreting that structure of knowledge as infinity does not eliminate the comparative aspect accompanying these affirmations. We notice that the tendency is to go beyond the human realm, and this is what transcendence implies. But attribution draws from human resources, too, and their self-interpretation.

★   ★   ★

A fundamental question that perforce arises in these expositions is whether the continuous analogy with the human realm is only an analogy or a sort of projection of human qualities onto the transcendent entity. This question cannot be ignored even if we do not take the view that the very affirmation of transcendent reality is a projection grounded in human or factual reality. The difference between the ontological position of the transcendent and its essence can be maintained where the essence is conceived as more akin to human essence and its self-awareness than the separation implied in the difference between the factual and the transcendent. A look at the history of the various meanings of divine attributes reinforces our appreciation of these various distinctions, in which the basic issue is whether attributes can be attributes of God precisely because they are related to human self-awareness. We cannot forget, for instance, the significant historical fact that the term "person" was introduced into the expositions of faith at a late stage of its terminological or philosophical interpretations. The basic meaning of "persona" as a mask or disguise may point not toward elucidating the nature of that which is affirmed in faith but to the introduction of an obscure aspect into the context. In addition, the concept of negative attributes prominent in medieval philosophy is a reinforcement, even terminologically speaking, of some of the hesitations regarding the application of attributes in this context because of the human field of association that is essential to it. Just the same, since faith is not knowledge—and with all the affinity between human beings and God, faith is not a divine intentionality but a human one—we are bound to come to the conclusion that the variations on the theme of the essence of the transcendent being as God are in the broad sense, at least, not unrelated to the human experience and its interpretations.

Let us refer at this point to Goethe, who says that when studying nature we are pantheists, when engaged in poetry, polytheists, and when acting as moral agents, monotheists. This statement implies that interpretations of the relation between reality and God are indeed interpretations of human experience and therefore are guided by a basic approach that is not necessarily of a religious character or grounded in faith. With all the evident differences, poetry as being congruous with polytheism is understood here as grounded in fantasy and therefore leading to a conception of differences within the encountered or experienced reality, that is, differences are expressed in the multiplicity of Godlike entities. But polytheism is not only an encounter with a multitude of events but an understanding of each embodiment of that multitude as of a supreme albeit limited power. The affinity between morality and monotheism is probably grounded in the interpretation of biblical monotheism as ethical monotheism. As such, it does not presuppose the autonomous character of morality but stresses morality as conduct, whatever its grounds; in the monotheistic direction they are grounded in commandments.

In any case, even if we take a critical view of the interpretation of these three attitudes regarding the ontological position of God, we may accept its implications: the interpretation of the transcendent being and its essence cannot be separated from the self-interpretation of the human experience even when a sublime or superlative connotation accompanies that move from the human to the divine realm. This is again one of those aspects that emphasize that faith is by definition grounded in human experience, though its *noema* is beyond and above that experience.

Having said this, I may now consider the move from faith to religion where religion is regarded as a more articulated and even institutionalized presentation of faith. Religion is an expression of faith. I shall deal with this issue after an intermediary step that will be concerned with the notion of holiness, which in its broad meaning can be considered an attribute, yet not a particular attribute like knowledge or justice and an attribute that possibly has no equivalent within human experience per se.

*   *   *

I conclude by recapitulating that the concept of the Absolute—or possibly the category implying that concept—is not applicable to immanent reality, which in terms of knowledge is the reality of relations. Empirical concepts are formed through knowledge or the apprehension of sense-data, and the background of time indicates the relational character of that reality. Yet the question is still open whether what is essential for the knowledge of immanent reality is applicable to that which is transcendent and contained in itself, as expressed in the term "thing in itself" or *causa sui,* when applied to the divine entity. Transcendence as a sphere may comprise all possible data of experience but in and of itself it is not involved in the relations between them. Faith, referring to transcendence as a sphere and as an entity, can thus not be subsumed under the character of knowledge, as the reality referred to in faith cannot be subsumed in the structure of immanent reality. We could say that this is faith proper. It is an awareness expressed in conjecture, but it is not knowledge. It refers to suprarelational reality, and, in many of its expressions, it is aware of its character. However, as indicated before, faith refers to truth, although the interpretation of the concept of truth here is probably closer to that which is essential to transcendence or closer to that which is its essence than to the principle of knowledge. This is possibly indicated in Jeremiah 10:10: "The Lord is the true God," where "true" or "truth" indicates that which is the essence of God, as the verse goes on to say: "He is the living God, and an everlasting king."

Indeed, the relation suggested by the image of the "living God" pertains in the direction from transcendent to immanent reality and not from the immanent to the transcendent. Within the scope of immanent reality, human beings pray and address themselves to the divine entity. But these manifestations of faith, although they occur within immanent reality and are events within it, are not events in the semiobjective sense of that term, as related to other events. The factual relation begins with the transcendent reality and reaches the fullness of its expression in creation and various expressions, such as *fons vitae,* emanation, or the unbroken flow between transcendent reality and that which is posited by it.

When I refer to the light posited within the human mind by the divine entity, I again refer to the transcendent end acting on the immanent setting. Thus, faith, even when not explicitly stressed by those who adhere to it and formulate it, is a sui generis awareness with a cognitive *element,* and yet it is not knowledge proper in the strict interpretation of the word. Again, the reference to the notion of truth may connote the constancy of the divine entity or its reliability. Reliability would be impossible, or it would be impossible to expect from the perspective of human beings, were not the divine entity constant and thus—again, from the human perspective—predictable and as such reliable; reliance is a human expectation referring to the constancy of the divine.

⋆   ⋆   ⋆

At this juncture, I ask whether faith is an irrational phenomenon since it cannot be taken as synonymous with rational knowledge and its manifestations. In many philosophical analyses of irrationality, we find the connection between understanding, as stating that something is irrational, and reason, which overcomes that statement and concurrently overcomes the characterization of irrationality. This is possible in the philosophical analysis because reason is conceived as manifesting a totality, and within the totality there is no room for something irrational, that is, something out of context, inexplicable, and so on. In the case of faith, we cannot follow this line of argument, because faith is not to be integrated, not even in reason, and thus we cannot take advantage of the category of totality. Hence, the distinction remains between knowledge—manifesting both understanding and reason—and faith. The question of the possible or alleged irrationality of faith therefore has to be dealt with as a separate problem. From the opposite end, if rationality connotes intelligibility, we may question whether rationality can be applied to the description or analysis of the phenomenon of faith, since transcendent reality as separated from relational reality is not to be subsumed under the description of intelligibility, once intelligibility is interpreted as referring to the context of relations.

Let me mention now some phenomena that have been characterized as irrational and in this context again ask whether faith is an irrational intentionality directed to an irrational realm. Two phenomena are most often referred to as irrational, the first being life. The presupposition seems to be that life proper cannot be rationally analyzed and brought completely under the purview of reason; it is just a given phenomenon or a given object and thus irrational. In addition, life may contain accidental aspects, and these cannot be classified or placed in a certain order since, being accidental, they contradict any order. The second phenomenon or object characterized as irrational is individual existence, which, because of its individuality, cannot be rationally integrated into any larger scheme. If we take these two phenomena—life and individuality—as paradigmatic for the sphere of irrationality, we are bound to come to the conclusion that transcendence as an object of faith cannot be integrated into these two different phenomena and again has to be seen as sui generis. Transcendence is not accidental since it is above or beyond the distinction between an order of relations, and something that deviates from that order as accidental. The distinction between order and accident is applicable only to immanent reality and not to the transcendent one. As to individuality, we must distinguish between what is individual—occurring just once and having distinctive features, as opposed to the features of the species—and the uniqueness of the divine entity. Even when we speak of the personal "essence" of God, the term is meant to emphasize the uniqueness and not the belonging to the category of human "persons." My conclusion is that neither transcendence nor the divine entity as the transcendent one can be regarded as phenomena that can be characterized as either rational or irrational.

As a phenomenon, transcendence has to be taken in its unique character, thus making any classification inapplicable. From the point of view of human intentionality, and here, from the point of view of faith, we are bound to come to the conclusion that faith as a correlate of transcendence is neither rational nor irrational. It must be seen as a phenomenon unto itself that has a cognitive dimension, but the knowledge it provides is of a special order, indeed, it cannot truly be considered knowledge, certainly not rational knowledge. Historically, we refer here again to the concept of *aseitas*.

At this juncture it might be possible to point to some affinity between faith and hypothesis, but this is rather problematic because of the various meanings of the notion of hypothesis. If we take it as in Francis Bacon's sense of being opposed to sensuous perceptions, faith can be understood as a hypothesis. But if we take hypothesis as connoting axioms, then faith cannot be understood as such. Neither can it be understood as a presupposition of some geometric or mathematical theorems, because faith is not a presupposition from which logical consequences are derived but rather is a noetic posture. If hypothesis is taken in its primary sense, that is, as an underlying assumption or promise, then we could say that transcendence and its affirmation are hypotheses because that which is affirmed "underlies" the immanent realm or the reality of the world. Here, too, there is no way of deducing what follows reality from that which "underlies" it, because what follows depends on an act and thus on an event.

Hence, I conclude—after making some suggestions as to the possible proximities between faith and various cognitive assumptions—that faith must be deemed a phenomenon sui generis, for transcendent reality has to be taken as a reality sui generis. The correlation between intentionality and its *noema* is retained as the outcome of this analysis. Still, faith is a manifestation of consciousness since it is a human phenomenon in spite of its transhuman direction.

Cognition and Reality: An Excursus

Conjecture is an affirmation of something. There is not—and in the case of faith there cannot be—any definite proof of that which is formulated or asserted in a conjecture. With respect to cognition in general, we distinguish between underlying awareness and that to which the awareness refers. This correlation applies also specifically to conjecture. Hence, by its very nature conjecture is an *intentional* act, whereas the *noema* is that to which the act refers. The correlation does not connote the possible consequence that there is a symmetry between the act—the *noesis*—and the *noema*, since in faith, as we shall see, the *noema* has preponderance and a supreme position.

Conjecture as surmise is an act of cognition expressed in the statement affirming the *noema* to which it refers. There can be different formulations of what is implied in the conjecture. These formulations do not change the basic character and the distinction between intentionality as such and the statement as confirmation.

To put it differently, we can see that the cognitive character of conjecture is a kind of acquaintance, not with that which we encounter, but with that which is referred to. Conjecture is a conclusion—even a vague one—and faith adheres to that conclusion and gives it a new direction.

The cognitive character of conjecture that leads to formulations—implying information or opinion about a state of affairs—is negatively expressed in our reflection on it in the first place as differing from construction. In a construction, we create a structure or an order. We bring together certain elements—as in classical philosophy—when some laws are considered as not given but constructed or created. That which is constructed may eventually have a structure of its own, like geometry or mathematics, but as a construction it is not an affirmation of that which is identified or discerned. The character of discourse applies to conjecture and thus to faith and therefore brings faith within the ambit of cognition. Conjecture is not an expression of fancy or imagination because it is not a creation. Faith is meant to refer to what is real though not given to apprehension by the senses. From this point of view, there might be an element of discovery inherent in faith as uncovering something not present to our senses but still conceived as present in reality.

*   *   *

From a negative or polemical angle, the characterization of a certain mode of faith as idolatry contains the conception that the objects worshiped are not real from the point of view of faith, though they might be real from a general point of view if, for instance, they are the stars or constellations. But the very term "idol" or "idolatry" employed in this context implies that there is no proper cognition of that which must be cognized in order to assume the position of what should be the adequate *noema* of faith. If idolatry has been interpreted as worshiping stars and constellations or wood and stones, it has been criticized for taking these sensuous objects as living realities to which one, in faith, may establish a relationship.

The conjunction of improper cognition and an improper object is suggested in various ways, such as the term "heathen," or *paganus,* both terms that point etymologically to those who dwell in a rural area and thus are "unenlightened." What is implied here is that faith is not just a commonsense awareness but intrinsically requires enlightenment, which does not necessarily connote erudition but still is above the simple level of ordinary apprehension of what is present in the world. When more elaborated categorical distinctions are made in criticizing idolatry as an improper expression of faith, idols are obviously understood as being nothing or as falsely isolating aspects of creation from their creator.

⋆　⋆　⋆

The cognitive basis of faith should be emphasized, although faith as *pistis* or *pietas* does contain a noncognitive dimension, an element of emotional immediacy that does not necessarily point to something given to awareness. Immediacy can also be interpreted as related to the lack of demonstration or proof characteristic of faith. In a more positive direction, faith as an integral whole (presupposing cognition expressed in awareness and affirmation) also contains the normative direction of these facets. It is understood as immediate, as opposed to that which is mediated and arrived at by way of a procedure of methodical steps that can often be defined. The difference between the object of cognition and the steps taken for the sake of that cognition is that the latter is, again, often accompanied by awareness.

Regarded as a form of cognition, faith refers to something beyond itself, or, to use a positional term, to an object. The object to which faith refers is understood as not given because it is not and cannot be encountered directly. The affirmation through faith of an object—not comprehended by the senses—as present, implies, of course, a distinction between that which is given and that which is present. In this double-faceted position of the object, one may probably discern certain features attributed to what theologians call transcendent and immanent reality. Thus, for example, the literature refers to the spiritual presence as different from the physical one, to the objective presence or the essential one, and ultimately also to use other terms from classical philosophy and theology that are significant precisely because they point to the difference between the given and present and that which is non-given and still present. These terms are "ubiquity" and *ens realissimum*. The latter, the real reality, is a realm totally other than reality or real objects within the immanent sphere. Terminologically, one has to observe that "reality" is related to *res*. One should perhaps question the transposition of a term, denoting objects *res*, to the sphere of transcendence or to a transcendent entity. The term "actuality," implying acting, thus might be more adequate in this context, but we cannot alter the established semantic usages. What we can do is call attention to the nuances that should be assumed and understood in our context. Negatively speaking, actuality or reality in general and also in the context of faith implies that which is not created or invented, that which is not contingent, being as it is, underlying all other modes of reality—whatever the meaning of the notion of underlying may be.

* * *

Before dealing with the distinction between levels of reality and the correlation between cognition and reality, it should be observed that the presence of the notion of God as *theos* became prominent in these elaborations of the conception of levels of reality, even in the appearance of the notion of pantheism. John Toland, who seems to have invented the term "pantheism," uses the conjunction *supremus deus*. Thus, he employs a distinction or grading regarding *deus* implied in the description *supremus*. We do not find, however, the term *theos* in Greek philosophy affirming the one and the whole. Hence, we can conclude that that term was introduced into the context of pantheism because of its major position in historical religions as pointing to a supreme reality as well as to perfection.

Here with pantheism, supreme reality and supreme perfection are understood as integrated in that reality, implying that a supremacy in terms of levels of reality is also supremacy in terms of norms or virtues. One of the etymological descriptions of *theos* relates that term to *theoria*, that is, seeing or visioning. God is understood as *theos*—as a being seeing everything.

★ ★ ★

It is appropriate in the context of reality—and the act of cognition intentionally directed toward it—to deal with truth as a principle related to faith as an affirmation. Truth is the principle guiding, or demanding that, the affirmation of a state of affairs should be adequate to that state—and here I use "adequate" not in the strict terminological sense applying to truth as adequacy, but in a broader sense as implying reference to that which is. In traditional religious texts, we find direct references to the notion of truth, such as in the Epistle to the Romans (2:20)—"the truth in the law"—or in 1 Corinthians (13:6)—". . . rejoiceth in the truth"—as opposed to the principle of equity. Truth may connote here that which is the proper meaning of law or that which is a proper cause for rejoicing. Thus, it possibly has not only a cognitive meaning but a meaning of that which, within the structure of the concepts dealt with, is the highest level of their realization. And, indeed, we also refer to this conjunction between truth and reality when we use expressions such as "he is a real artist," implying that "real" connotes the full expression or manifestation of that which is the essence of the sphere referred to, such as, for instance, art. Truth may mean fulfillment here—in connection with what is real—and thus in the sphere of reality may connote levels of reality. The employment of the terms "reality" or "suprareality" may perhaps be explained from this point of view.

With respect to the concept of "reality" and its position within the sphere of faith, we may turn to Johann Friedrich Herbart (1776–1841). Herbart began his presentation of reality as an absolute position, his point of departure being something that is empirically given and yet contains some basic contradictions. For instance, we say that a thing is a unity and yet contains a plurality, that it is constant and yet fluid, and so forth. The way to overcome these contradictions, according to Herbart, is to surmount the variety of predicates—that is, the variety of features or qualities—

and refer to their absolute position. The absoluteness of that position implies that it contains no relation to any other position, or, put positively, that it points utterly to what is contained in itself. So reconciled, these components, Herbart held, are essentially what we mean by "reality."

In much of our cognitive concern, we deal with the position and not with qualities. For instance, and I refer here to an example given by Herbart, when we think about the immortality of the soul, we consider the very position of the soul and not its qualities. That position, therefore, corresponds to the basic questions of our cognitive concern. The answer to those questions is yes or no, where the yes refers to the absolute position. (The usual conception that reality bears qualities has led to the notion that the subject of those qualities is part of the absolute position.) That absolute position leads to the conclusion that I suggested earlier—that real things are different from those that are only present in our thinking, since the latter are part and parcel of "the free game" of thinking and do not contain the decisive component of resisting any attempt to disregard or deny them. Thus, the absolute position is, on the one hand, that which underlies perceptible features and qualities and, on the other, that which we encounter and do not invent.[1]

Rudolf Hermann Lotz (1817–1881) took the opposite view in this controversy, criticizing the conception that reality can be understood as an absolute position lacking any connections and relations to anything beyond itself. His position was that if something is without any connections, it is nonreal. Something can be real only within a context. There is also a connection between our sensations and that which is real, though sensations can lead us to mistakes in our assertion of that which is real. Here again, the givenness is exposed to a critical analysis that leads to the conception that something separated or excluded and existing in its own sphere solely unto itself cannot be considered real.[2] This contro-

1. Johann Friedrich Herbart formulated his conception in many of his writings. See especially his *Lehrbuch zur Einleitung in die Philosophie* (1813).

2. Rudolf Hermann Lotz stated his conception of reality as context in several of his major writings. Perhaps one of the clearest statements is in his book *Mikrokosmos* (1856; 1864), 9, chap. 1.

versial issue, whose axis is whether reality is something that has empirical context or something that can be separated from a context and conceived in and of itself, is of relevance for the position of reality from the point of view of faith. From a different point of view, this brings us to the distinction between levels of reality: that which is considered to be real in the empirical context may have a functional or relational meaning, whereas that which is considered to be real in the realm of transcendence may only be grasped by concepts.

*   *   *

The presence of a cognitive component in faith cannot overshadow the difference between faith and knowledge. Faith remains within the scope of conjecture and thus does not develop methods to judge or validate itself. It is close from this viewpoint to *sensus communis,* which is—in Vico's view—an insight into the probable. It does not necessarily lead to common consent, but it may. It is probably not by chance that Franz Rosenzweig related his interpretation of faith to what he called *Understanding the Sick and Healthy* (1953). The original German title of this volume is *Der gesunde und kranke Menschenverstand (Healthy and sick common sense).* The affinity between faith and common sense (that is, ordinary human understanding) can be maintained, though it does not necessarily refer to transcendence. For faith is here rather an attitude and not a cognitive orientation.

It is apposite here to cite Charles Sanders Peirce: "Belief is not a momentary mode of consciousness; it is a habit of mind enduring for some time . . . and, like other habits, it is perfectly self-satisfied." Peirce accordingly coined the phrase "the fixation of belief," and one could say that religions are either fixations of belief or instruments in its service.[3]

---

3. Charles Sanders Peirce, *The Fixation of Belief.* Both quoted passages are included in *The Philosophy of Peirce: Selected Writings,* ed. J. Buchler (London: Routledge & Kegan Paul, 1950).

CHAPTER EIGHT

Holiness

I will now present some of the concepts that have been attributed to the position of being as "absolute." Again, it is not suggested that these predicates are inherent in the attitude of faith. They have been introduced into the description of faith in its relation to the divine entity—influenced by certain conceptual attempts—not detached from the basic meaning of absoluteness. Among those concepts, that of holiness occupies a special position because holy or holiness in its various formulations connotes that which is separated. The sacred—sanctity—*hagios,* or *kodesh,* is meant to stress the position of being apart and thus inaccessible, totally separated, enclosed, and so forth. In this sense, the notion of holiness attributed to transcendence carries more the character of articulation than of predication. In addition, we find the notion not only expressed linguistically in various terms but also rather widely diffused in different religious expressions. Thus, for instance, "taboo" is sacred in the sense that it is placed apart from any common access. From this point of view, "taboo" may have a more negative connotation, pointing to something harmful or even dangerous to human beings and something that has to be kept separate, utterly apart. The notion of *mana* connotes something exceptional and, as such, full of impact and effect. The line of demarcation between that which is holy and that which is before or beyond it is inherent in its various expressions. Therefore, what is described as profane—related to *pro fanus*—points to places that are before the *fanum,* that is to say, outside the holy place.

Hence, we do not find, and understandably so, interpretations of God that emphasize the absolutely separated position of God and employ the predicate of holiness. To be sure, Spinoza's interpretation of God as being absolutely infinite—as the substance consisting of infinite attributes, each of which expresses eternal and infinite essentiality—differs from the conception emphasizing God's separateness. The corollary component of Spinoza's definition is that God is the "indwelling" and not the transient cause of all things. God as "indwelling" cannot be conceived as separated, and thus there is no anchor or basis for the attribution of holiness to God in that interpretation.

★   ★   ★

We encounter here a paradoxical aspect in the interpretation of holiness and its position in terms of absoluteness as separation. Holiness is bestowed on places or festivals, and thus its separated position dwells in some parts of the factual world. These parts are not holy in themselves or on their own; holiness is brought into them. Nevertheless, the separated aspect of holiness is not strictly preserved once holiness dwells in factual occurrences or things. Thus, in spite of the basic affinity between separateness and holiness, holiness is introduced into the scope of immanent reality, which is not the case with eternity and the other variations on the theme of absoluteness. It is probably difficult to expound the "inner logic" of that shift from the transcendent realm to the immanent one unless we assume that holiness, in spite of its separateness, has a sort of igniting or even emanating capacity that leads to the self-transcendence of transcendence in a direction "below" itself. The other aspect—so prominent in the Bible—of the similarity between human beings and God, expressed in the command "Be holy because I am holy," is not only of an "igniting" character, since it implies a norm and a permanent one. Thus, it may be cognate to the aspect of commandment or revelation. Revelation in this case is not of a word transmitted to human beings, but of a content related to the transcendent entity; it is based on the possible similarity to, or imitation of, human beings to God addressing them. Parenthetically, we should observe that when Hegel uses the notion "holy,"[1] he interprets it as pointing to the total harmonization of reality and thus as connoting the comprehensive totality against particularity.

The presence of the normative aspect in the notion of holiness may lead us to discern an additional feature of the concept, namely, the totality of all its possible predicates.[2] Unlike attributes such as wisdom or justice, which are related to the differentiations present in human beings, holiness is meant to indicate the comprehensive togetherness of all the qualities as Rudolph Otto rightly stressed. This togetherness is essentially the total coalescence of the aspect of reality and the aspect of its qualitative descriptions. Hence, holiness can be understood as wholeness. The full harmony of the different components of holiness is present even in Kant's concept of the holy will where there is no discrepancy whatsoever between will and the norm guiding it, in contrast to the human sphere where what can be achieved is but good will and not holy will.

⋆   ⋆   ⋆

However, all these aspects do not exhaust the full meaning or impact of the concept of holiness. This must be emphasized in spite of its component of presentness in some fragments of factual reality. Holiness may also be considered sublimity, which again can be understood merely as an explication of separateness. Two additional, contradictory aspects are deemed to be inherent in holiness; on the one hand, it fascinates—it attracts—human beings, calling upon them to approach it. On the other hand, holiness is regarded as tremendous, beyond the scope of attracting and even causing fear and awareness of the distance between human beings and itself. These two aspects of holiness, different as they are, make it an aspect of the divine entity that evokes in human beings a desire to express their relation to it. This latter aspect is present in various ritual acts and in prayer.

1. G. W. F. Hegel, *Ethics,* Pt. 1, "Concerning God," definition 7.
2. Ibid. proposition VIII.

I will now consider the ceremonial expressions related to faith, being aware, even more than before, that these components are inherent in religions and not in faith proper. Hence, the first question I ask at this juncture is, What leads faith to religion, without assuming a simple continuity between the two? Or, to put it differently, What turns faith as an attitude into religion qua institution? It is appropriate to point here that religions apply the notion of holiness to different dimensions of existence, and tend to attribute the relation of those "secondary" manifestations of holiness to its primary status. One of the primary derivations of the concept of holiness is the introduction of the concept of glory, which applies to God but also to his manifestations in nature and in human existence.[3] Glory connotes an invisible essence, although it is present in the visible. The difference between holiness as implying separation and glory as connoting manifestation is probably the major difference between the two concepts. Glory presupposes holiness. The German term *Herrlichkeit* is related to *Herr* and thus to "mastery"—whereas "mastery" inherently refers to those who are obedient.

★   ★   ★

The attribution of holiness to the transcendent being or God is an interpretation of his position as totally different and thus separated from immanent or human reality. The normative aspect of that position is meant to reinforce his transcendence. It stands above the attributes even more so since attributes cannot be separated from human experience or from human self-reflection.

Still, we find in the history of thought, or in the "climate of opinion," a kind of employment of the notion of holiness in the opposite direction, when the notion of sanctity of life became common. To be sure, in Plato's *Phaedo* we find the attribution of eternity to life, but that attribution applies to the idea of life and not life as a given or even sensuous reality. Holiness is applied not to the idea of

---

3. Hegel, *Philosophische Propadeutik*, in *Werke*, ed. Glockner, 3:98.
4. Plato, *Phaedo*, 106d.

life but—if at all—to life as reality in the immanent sense or to the life of human beings. There cannot be any doubt that we encounter here a transposition of a concept from the transcendent sphere to the immanent one. There might exist several reasons or motivations for that transposition: one of them is probably that the very notion of life evokes an unconditional respect or even reverence. This response to holiness—of respect or reverence—is the tertium quid, explaining to some extent this transposition. The attribution of sanctity to life cannot be considered to be based on a philosophically systematic argument. Hence, it does not imply the denial of the realm of transcendence and its holiness. It leads to a vague coexistence of the attribute applied to the two spheres. Respect does not necessarily refer to glory.

★   ★   ★

The move from faith, as an underlying attitude and conviction, to certain feelings can be understood as a continuation of faith and, by the same token, as its interpretation. As interpretation, it is manifold because reverence and love cannot be considered identical but partial—and thus plural—interpretations of the underlying position. Still, feelings, cognitive as they are, are within the inner scope of human beings, while cults, rituals, and so forth, are external expressions, related to acts and deeds. Acts and deeds in cults cannot be separated from acts and deeds in cultures, and it is not by accident that the two words—cults and culture—relate to the same root. Expressions as acts and deeds, however, can be understood in the broadest sense, as for instance in Dharma where morals, customs, law, and rituals are brought into the larger scope of human conduct in general and its various manifestations. Cults can be understood—in a more limited way—as visible socially organized modes of expression meant to be grounded in faith and mediated through the various feelings expressing faith. The external aspect of cults cannot be ignored, for we are dealing here with

5. The variations of the notion of sanctity of life are dealt with in Nathan Rotenstreich, *Man and His Dignity* (Jerusalem: Magnes Press, 1983), pp. 191 ff.

performances, solemnly executed; there is always a possibility that the external expression, even when intended to give shape to an attitude, will become a semi-independent realm. A case in point is language, which is meant to express meanings or judgments, but as soon as the reservoir of expressions exists, it has its own standing and momentum. Even when—as in the context of Dharma, and also in Tao—the modes of conduct are meant to be the external expression, the possibility of a semiseparation of the cults is, to say the least, more conceivable than the separation of feelings. One might suggest that cults, whatever their foundation, are a mode of festivity and, as such, like clothing. Indeed, the introduction of that analogy is not arbitrary because festive behavior is very often performed in special garments.

I wish to emphasize an additional aspect of cults, namely, that of service or worship. Worship expresses the attitude of reverence and thus is accompanied by gestures of tribute or homage. In this case, reliance on human or interhuman experience is relevant since interrelations between human beings paying homage implies maintaining a distance and expressing that distance not only in words but also in specific deeds. If this is indeed the case within interhuman relations, it is clearly more so in the relation between human beings and the transcendent being, where distance is inherent and the issue is to find a proper act that appropriately can express the distance and at the same time express the human attempt to pay homage to that distant, transcendent reality. Thus sacrifice, for instance, which is a ritual act revolving around certain intentions and certain instrumental aspects, is one of the possible manifestations of service and homage. Cults are considered holy or sacred in themselves because of their reference to holiness. Thus their holiness may be said to be secondary or derivative. But the secondary aspect becomes self-contained to some extent, once it is viewed not only with respect to attitudes but also to the *noema* of those attitudes.

In cultic worship, we find not only religious service and rite but also some expectations on the part of those involved. Thus, for instance, reverence is a one-sided attitude of human beings toward God. In worship, expectation of a response from God is manifest in the expressions used, articulating, for instance, desire for divine forgiveness or forbearance. Worship is thus two-sided, that is, a human attitude and a desired response from God. Whitehead observed that rituals generate emotions; as I have tried to show, rituals are also meant to express emotions.

The social character of religious rites, unlike the individual character of feelings and sentiments, makes it possible for them to be related to public or historic events such as, for example, in the case of Passover, which seeks to preserve the memory of the Exodus from Egypt. Here, the mediation of ritual, as commemorative, should again be stressed since the events recalled were visible public occurrences. As such, they may call for a commemoration that acknowledges their social or historical character. Here, too, the issue of whether the commemorative aspect of the ritual evokes emotions or remains within the "open scene" is a question, and no unequivocal answer is possible. With all due differences, the same consideration applies to what is known as "rites of passage," such as ceremonies related to birth or death. These events are visible and open, and even when they take place within the purely individual sphere, they are still social events. The ritualistic aspect is meant to give emphasis to the social component of these events, which, in spite of their individuality, are related to the realm of social acts.

Despite the relation between cults and the underlying emotions informing them, they are also marked by an inherent estrangement from emotions; hence, we may understand why cults often seem to become merely ceremonial, formal, and outward. It is always possible—historically this is the case—that this tendency of cult evokes protests and attempts to restore the attitude of faith to its inner core, as with Pietism in the development of Christianity or even Protestantism in reaction to Catholicism.

Cults seek to express devotion but also anticipate benevolent response from the object of worship. From a historical or anthropological perspective, some cults possess the components of magic. This is so since cult practice is conceived not only as requesting divine favor but also as influencing the divine. This intended influence should be interpreted against the background of a close relation between man and the power of the divine. Thus, what goes by the term "theurgic" influence—namely, the expectation to communicate with spirits so as to influence them—is not an essential component of rituals or cults but can within the context of various cultures be regarded as sometimes belonging to them.

★   ★   ★

I have considered cults as acts and deeds expressed in ceremonies. However, there is an additional cultic component related in words: prayer. It goes without saying that prayers are linguistic expressions, though they can be accompanied by gestures and are occasionally totally immersed in them. I here wish to consider the verbal expression of prayer, whose relation to cult is manifest in what may be called its inherent dimension of expectation.

Prayers are part of the cult or ritual. Terminologically, such prayers are referred to as "litany," a term that stresses the public character of prayers and thus their position as a part of the ritual. There is also "liturgy," which has a different emphasis. Here I refer to the etymological root of the term, viz., *ergos,* which relates prayer to the magical aspect of cult since liturgical prayer is related to its effect.

Language is both a vehicle of expression and medium of liturgical prayer—that is to say, in prayer, the component of mediation is implied between human beings and the divine entity. Even when prayers are accompanied by somatic gestures, like kneeling or bowing—and note that the Hebrew word *beracha* (blessing, prayer) is related to *berech,* "knee"—their linguistic component or essence turns prayers into self-contained expressions.

Prayer, like blessing, is directed in the first place to the divine entity. As such, it expresses the affirmation of the divine entity through the medium of language, adding to that affirmation not only the assertion that the entity is there but also that it has an impact on the reality of the world, including that of human beings. "Blessing"—an English rendering of the Latin *benedicare*—connotes by virtue of its root term the good (*bene*); the attribution of goodness to the divine entity confirmed or affirmed in prayer is accompanied by the expectation that that entity will be benevolent to human beings.

In this context, an additional aspect of blessing has to be mentioned, expressed in the statement the Hebrew benediction: "Blessed be the judge of truth," which is pronounced in the context of a funeral or over a person who has died. Here, the blessing is the affirmation of justice inherent in the divine entity and not of his anticipated benevolence. Yet, the emphasis on justice indicates that death lies within the broad context of divine goodness. I distinguish here between goodness—which is either a component of justice or identical with it—and benevolence, which is an anticipated attitude of God in his relations toward concrete human beings. Prayers that affirm God's justice and inherent goodness are thus to be distinguished from prayers that express an anticipation or hope of God's benevolent acts to come.

In any case, prayer makes manifest the two poles of faith: the attitude of human beings, and the position of God. This is so even when the divine entity is a "being" and not a "personal entity," with all due reservations about the employment of that term. The human aspect of prayer becomes particularly prominent in the modes of asking or beseeching inherent in some directions of prayer. The form of beseeching or petition is not confined to the acknowledgment of the divine entity but contains an expectation of a specific response. Accordingly, in prayer, we encounter both praise or adoration of the divine entity, and the power of God to respond. Prayer is thus a conjunction of thanking and acknowledging the unique power of God. In Hebrew, the term is *lehodot*, which expresses thanks and acknowledging. Since it is expressed in a single term, the conjunction of the two aspects is brought out more clearly. From the point of view of the divine entity, prayer is directed toward the integration of power and goodness as the warrant for the fulfillment of the expectation.

There is an additional possible direction in prayer, related to the human situation—namely, failure or sin, asking for forgiveness, and thus presupposing the confession expressed in prayer. In order to ask forgiveness, one must confess that something evil has been done. That evil is a transgression not only of moral rules but also of rules depending on or ordained by the divine entity. Thus, prayer in this direction contains a confession of transgression and the presupposition that the person who committed the transgression is accountable for his or her deeds. Transgression contradicts the divine commandment and thus is contrary to pleasing God. Prayer is intended to ask God for forgiveness. It contains the obligation not to repeat the deed of transgression and thus to be worthy of divine benevolence, not only as forgiving but also as responding to the expectation in the positive sense of a new situation endowed with goodness. There are specific occasions that are marked by prayers and blessings, especially those that allow for a conjunction between rites of passage and blessings, for instance, at the birth of a child or a wedding. These occasions are understood as turning points in human biography and, as such, are considered congenial to expressing expectations and asking for God's blessing.

In these variations of prayer, it should be emphasized that, although articulated in language, prayer is not a proposition in the logical sense of the term. As a linguistic statement, prayer also reflects a measure of human self-awareness and its dependence on the expected response. We cannot assume that prayer in this sense is a manifestation of utter dependence on the divine entity, because, after all, it is an expression of human beings within the context of their own existence. Prayer is an important manifestation of faith, combining human awareness and intentionality. The cultic aspect becomes prominent with the codification of prayers; that they are formulated in a general way applicable to possible individual situations or sentiments. This makes prayer into what is called "constant" and thus may sometimes even be criticized because of the possible estrangement from the particularities of the singular individual conditions and the individual agents. Yet this aspect again cannot be disconnected from the medium of language because language, though meant to allow for individual expression, occurs within a common texture, which can be understood, at least partially, as estranged from the individual here and now. Nonetheless, as they become common coin, prayers are not poetry—they are not individual expressions of the common language—though to be sure prayer, especially in its liturgical form, often incorporated poetry.

By way of summary, I underscore that, although prayers express expectations with respect to God's actions, the expectations are within the human context. To put it bluntly, God does not pray to himself. There are, as we have explored before, attributes that can be part of the human condition and still be understood as predicates of the divine entity. However, there are certain acts that are exclusively of a divine character, such as creation and revelation. Prayers presuppose the particularities of the human condition, directing human beings in their concrete situations to the divine entity. Through language as a medium, that direction attains explicit prominence—that is, linguistically—and not only ceremonially or symbolically, as is characteristic of the cult in general.

I shall now turn to an additional aspect of cults that finds its manifestation in the reference to space and time and not media, namely, festivities and feasts.

$\star$ $\quad$ $\star$ $\quad$ $\star$

Cults are sums total of acts and deeds that are extensively prescribed by established codes. Hence, there is possible tension between the intention or consciousness and the actual performance of the cultic acts. Further, by their very nature these acts occur in time and space. They are, like any act, an intervention in factual reality that aims to shape that reality in accordance with the meaning and expectations inscribed in those acts. The attitudes expressed in these acts occur on the human level, while expectations are intended toward the divine and as such their results are not assured. There is no parallelism between the ontological position of the transcendent being understood as perduring and the constancy of cultic acts, which by definition remain intrinsically bound to the human situation. Acts, even those of a cultic character, are sporadic and possibly erratic and in this sense cannot be constant, at least inasmuch as the underlying feeling is perforce one of their inherent components. The shift toward cults is meant to overcome the sporadic, not to mention erratic character of human deeds.

The structural character of cultic acts becomes significant also in the fact that some of them refer to the comprehensive dimensions of reality, that is, space and time, and not to that which is actually included in those dimensions. These comprehensive dimensions are invested with interpretations of holiness by certain cultic acts and are therefore considered to reflect the transcendent position of holiness and its normative meaning. There is an implied presupposition in this direction of cultic acts that points to the parallelism between the comprehensive character of dimensions and transcendence. In some trends of Greek philosophy, space and time are interpreted as images of eternity; later, Newton spoke of space as a *sensorium dei* in order to emphasize the "intermediary status of space" between God and the factual encountered reality.

Indeed, when it is claimed that certain terrestrial objects such as mountains or stones and trees are holy, a *sensorium dei* is meant. These cultic interpretations of space imply not that God comprehends everything and, as such, is space himself but, rather, they imply that delineated parts of space are understood as filled with the presence of God. Therefore, they are holy places, and pilgrimages, in essence a cultic act, are undertaken to reach them. Since the component of journey or travel is inherent in pilgrimage, the move in space assumes a cultic character; the means are as cultic as is the end. Broadly speaking, the framework of reality qua space is invested with meanings and, in this case, not meanings like expectation or atonement, but meaning in the most supreme interpretation as holiness. Obviously, pilgrimages take place in time, and thus we encounter here the conjunction between the components of space and time.

A further step in the direction of investing cultic meanings in space is expressed by building temples, where space is both the comprehensive framework and the specific land for the edifice. Temples can be considered holy in themselves but also as enabling ceremonial conduct that expresses the attitude toward holiness. Therefore notice that space provides the broad framework for interpreting some objects as sacred. It goes without saying that fetishism is essentially grounded in the interpretation of space in this direction, even when we cannot assume that that interpretation is explicit in the fetishistic cults.

The fragmentary approach to the broad framework is paralleled in the relation to some fragments of time, most strikingly manifested in "holy days," as they are called in some languages. In Hebrew, there is no parallel term; what are considered "holidays" are either called "good days" or "days of awe." The relation to fragments of time, but also to parts of space, becomes prominent in sacrifices performed at certain prescribed times and at certain prescribed places, such as temples. In some languages, holidays are characterized as days of leisure, apparently in order to emphasize the separation from daily life and to stress the release from involvement in everyday existence. The continuity of time is therefore open to intervention or interpretation by the cultic approach, making some days or fragments of time absorb meanings related to transcendence. Bringing those meanings into everyday existence is effected by the recitation of prayers or by following a prescribed order of eating, as well as adhering to rules governing what is permitted and what is forbidden to eat. The obvious presupposition is that eating is an everyday necessity, but it has to be guided by cultic prescriptions.

The broad reference to time becomes prominent in an additional component sometimes grounded in faith—namely, the eschatological expectation, which in itself is not of a cultic character. It does not call for acts here and now, except possibly for those in any case prescribed by cults. Eschatology refers to a total meaning of the "end of time," with "end" in the teleological sense, for instance, as redemption or salvation. It further presupposes that the investment of fragments of time with the meaning of holiness is not sufficient because fragments of time cannot replace the totality and its awaited end. Salvation or redemption may mean separation from the everyday character of human reality. There is here, by definition, a relation to time. For eschatology connotes redemption not as a move toward transcendence but as possibly a most perfect manifestation of transcendence within the broadest and most comprehensive dimension of human reality. Because time is the dimension of changes, and these may eventually reach the end, time in this sense seems to be more congruous with the expectations of faith than space. Space is the dimension of static reality, while time is the dimension of dynamic reality and thus may bring about the heightened expectations, guided by faith and grounded in it. Here again we encounter the aspect of attitude of expectation, which is such an essential element of faith. Since eschatology is the focus of this expectation, we find an additional manifestation of the basic feature of faith, that is, that the expectation is there but its fulfillment is beyond the scope of expectation, in the individual realm as the response of God to prayer, as well as in the universal realm as the fulfillment of the end of history as salvation.

One conclusion that can be reached in this context is that in faith there is a tension between human intentionality—which among its other manifestations includes expectation—and divine grace. There can be no proof of the meeting between expectation and its fulfillment, because proof would turn the fulfillment into a part of factual human reality and thus paradoxically erase the transcendent, divine source of the fulfillment. Before reaching some additional conclusions, one may already state that faith is based on a conviction that cannot be demonstrated in spite of recurrent efforts made to do so—for instance, the various proofs of the existence of God. This dialectical situation will be our concern in one of the following chapters.

Having stressed the semisuperior position of time in faith and thus its more abstract character, I shall deal with an additional component of faith as related to time, namely, the historical dimension, not in terms of the end but in terms of the process. I am referring to the position of tradition in faith and some of the aspects relevant to the interaction between the two. Here, too, I deal with faith and religion.

CHAPTER NINE

Active Expressions of Faith

The statement in the Epistle to the Hebrews (11:1–3) is an appropriate point of departure for the next part of this analysis: "Now faith is the assurance of things hoped for, the conviction of things not seen. For by it man of old received divine approval. By faith we understand that the world was created by the word of God, so that what is seen is made out of things which do not appear."

Several cognitive aspects of faith are emphasized here, such as conviction, understanding, and the implied relation between things seen and those unseen. Since conviction is cited as a characteristic of faith, one would be entitled—paradoxically as it may seem—to introduce some aspects of the Socratic approach into this analysis. That is to say, inherent in faith is the knowledge that we do not know. This Socratic assumption is present in the feature of faith as the assurance or conviction of certain things or events, although they are not "seen." That which is seen is related to that which is unseen, asserting the impact of the unseen on the seen. The component of hope is obviously significant, but it relates to expectations and not to the awareness of things and their relations. Divine creation as such does not imply the realization of hope; it only points to the realm where that realization can take place. In addition, in Socrates' view, we find that the attitude of the person in search of knowledge is expressed in given attitudes, such as care. Hence, when we attempt to apply this exposition to the basic awareness of faith, we are led to various distinctions that have been emphasized in the different descriptions of faith. I will start with what can be characterized as a state of mind, and I shall distinguish between it and what can perhaps be properly characterized as active feelings, though the line of demarcation between the two is rather fluid.

When faith refers to something unseen, asserting its overwhelming impact on that which is seen, and when, moreover, the person who through faith is "aware" of the unseen is by the same token aware of his own basic position, then that awareness implies a personal self-evaluation of one's position in the order of existence. The comparison that I expounded in the previous analysis leads to a self-evaluation that can be characterized as humility. Humility may imply restraint, including self-restraint, modesty, and in general the awareness that human existence and the reality to which it belongs are not on the level of primary reality, leading to a rejection of attempts to overstep that which is delineated by that awareness. Humility thus leads to the rejection or criticism of vanity and, in general, of that which is called *hubris* in Greek. The affirmation of human beings as images only implies that awareness and its additional expressions may all lead to the ongoing affirmation of the distance between man and God once the concept of God is introduced into the frame of reference of this analysis.

The "awareness" borne by humility contains an active component, although it is more in the background than manifest in particular expressions. Those expressions are to be found in some active feelings, which can be described paradoxically as cognitive, since they cannot be separated from an awareness of the distance emphasized above. Indeed, when the concept of God is introduced, faith proper can be conceived as an illumination originating in God; the very attitude is already a manifestation of the divine intervention in human existence. Still, if we consider the conception of the Upanishads, whereby God does not proclaim himself but is in everyone, there is no reliance on intervention; self-awareness implicitly contains a reference to God.

Nevertheless, what goes by the broad term "piety" is an active expression of the basic attitude of faith, and in that expression we find a conjunction of several components that are not at all identical and to some extent that even contradict each other. Piety comprises the awareness of distance, reverence, evaluation of the supreme or of that which is above us, thanksgiving, expectation of response, and, in general, those acts of cognitive feelings that are manifestations of devotion. The various expressions are inner acts that refer to the divine entity. They contain an element related to the presence of God, not only as the *noema* of our intentionalities but as granting us a relation to the divine entity. At the same time, some inner expressions are present—and in this sense I refer to Paul Tillich's correlation of the "theonomous" and "autonomous" elements of faith. There is a human response to divine reality, and that response may take the shape of, for instance, listening and obedience but also of love, although the attitude of love is probably but a transposition from interhuman relations to the relation between man and God. The two aspects stressed before are present in the attitude of love: *amor* is the motivation on the part of the human being, while *caritas* is the response on behalf of the divine entity. Therefore, in the various attitudes, we find a required response from the human end and an assumed—hoped for—response on the part of the divine. Neither of these attitudes is simply given; we are called on, or call on ourselves, to develop these attitudes in order to reach a position adequate to the underlying position of faith. Awareness of that which is above the human order gains expression in the attitude of reverence because the revered object is regarded as exalted, sublime, and sacred.

Humility can be considered a background condition even when we do not interpret it in terms of the natural corruption of human beings, original sin, and so forth. What can be said is that the introduction of notions like "natural corruption" is an interpretation of that state of affairs that in more neutral terms is described as evoking humility. In addition, I should mention that the attitude of reverence—probably originally more congruous with the attitude of faith—was transferred to the realm of ethics and understood, as in Kant, as reverence for moral law or, in a broader sense, as reverence for life in general.

★   ★   ★

Earlier in this analysis, I dealt with the transition from the broad attitude of faith to some more specific attitudes expressed not only on the level of awareness but also on the level of motivations for more concrete human acts as they can be seen within the scope of devotion. These are expressions that by and large remain within that which can be called "inner attitudes." Yet I find that faith is expressed not only in those attitudes, but in certain more visible modes of behavior as well, such as rituals.

Conviction, it would seem, is bound to be expressed not only in sentiments but also in acts. To be sure, this is not always so because a conviction may find adequate manifestation within its own terms. But faith is apparently one of those convictions that inevitably seeks external expression. In the first place, it is an attitude assumed by one particular human being but at the same time recognized as pertaining also to other human beings. Thus, a tacit communication follows the attitude of faith.

If expressions are to follow conviction, one could say that there is no limit to such expressions: faith is not confined to sentiments or attitudes but goes beyond them to sacrifices, feasts, and so on. This has to be said already at this point, even assuming that cognitive feelings are more inner clues to the basic attitude than ceremonial expressions are. In addition, one could say that, since faith is a conviction that, as such, cannot be justified by proofs or warranted by evidence, it achieves as it were some compensation by expressing itself in certain modes of behavior and these are by definition of a more social character than the "inner" attitudes of feelings, cognitive as they may be. Thus, I find that faith becomes not only a conviction but also a sum total of acts to be recognized with all the problematic aspects that go with it.

CHAPTER TEN

From Generation to Generation

The parallelism between the respective approaches to space and to time is manifest in the investment of specific places and days with holiness. The parallelism is clear in the Latin terms *religiose loca* and *religiosae dies.* Places are given, while fragments of time are considered to be related to events and are not primarily given. Because of certain occurrences, holiness is assigned to events, and the days associated with them are deemed holy. Events that do not have a meaning within the scope of faith may evoke festivities, but these are not assumed to be related to holiness.

The interpretation of time from the standpoint of faith has an additional significance, and the structural differences between space and time become evident in this context. Time is the framework of both succession and duration.[1] Succession as encompassing ongoing events can be seen as given or presupposed. Children, of course, arrive after their parents; succession is inherent in the relation. Moreover, succession is of a formal character inherent in time as such. Succession is the background of continuity, implying sequence. Whether those who succeed are aware of their position as subsequent is not an aspect of succession but one of human self-awareness and thus of interpretation. There are imposed sequences, such as the biological one, but there are also accepted sequences such as the reception of language, which comes from

1. On the aspects of time, see Nathan Rotenstreich, "Between Succession and Duration," *Kant-Studien* (1990), pp. 211 ff.

the preceding generation and is received by the following ones. At this point, I touch on the component of duration essential to the nature of time. Duration implies that something like a content endures or persists in succession and in spite of it. The genes persist in the organ. In the historical sphere, language continues to exist and is the background and medium of expression coming from the previous generation and continues to operate in the subsequent one. While succession is related to time as a form, duration is related to both form and content. Containing a content in that which is transmitted to the succeeding generation may have an archeological meaning as a relic of the past maintained in that dimension. But it may have an impact on the succeeding generations, and, here again, language is a case in point. No individual invents a language, and no generation invents a language. Language is and can be a medium of communication because it is understood and thus preexists for the generation concerned. The line of demarcation between that which is accepted and that which is acknowledged as binding or guiding is obviously rather thin. This aspect of faith will preoccupy us in the forthcoming analysis.

The phenomenological difference between space and time—and the impact of that difference on the attitude of faith—becomes salient also for time as a linear development. We already noticed the manifestation of faith in relation to the future—more specifically as the eschatological end is grounded in the attitude of expectation and hope inherent in faith. But the attitude to the past is nevertheless characteristic of at least some manifestations of faith, possibly because faith does not interpret itself as instantaneous or even as spontaneous without preceding resources or examples. Faith interprets itself, not as inventing itself, but as present in the forefront of the basic human situation in its relation to the facticity of the world. Hence, the continuous attempt to relate to the past and to bring the past into faith—here and now—seems, at least to some extent, to belong to the essence of faith. This relation becomes prominent in the position of tradition—in the context of faith—as the continued legacy from the past to the present, evoking acceptance by the present generation of that which is brought into its horizon from the past. The past as given and thus belonging to facticity lies within the horizon of faith.

★ ★ ★

The term *traditio* has undergone changes in usage. Originally, it connoted a transmission from one person to another, with the two coexisting. It connoted the material transmission of objects or the transmission of the right to use an object; even the term for transmitting money is to be found in the original sources (*pecuniam tradit*). This original meaning—as applying to coexisting persons—changed when tradition became invested with the meaning of handing over from one generation to another, implying both the process of transmitting and the content transmitted, as well as the enduring nature of that which is transmitted. In the first place, tradition connoted oral tradition: persons of one generation taught that which is transmitted to the following generation. Indeed, one of the primary meanings of tradition in this sense relates to the transmission of biblical or scriptural texts. In the case of the Hebrew Bible, where there are only consonants and no vowels, the transmission taught those who received it how to read the text—the significance of this has been rightly stressed in Franz Joseph Molitor's book on tradition.[2] Due to this relation to the biblical text, tradition already acquires a meaning in terms of faith or religion. But we cannot confine ourselves only to the historical background of the acceptance of the term "religion" into the context of faith. We must ask whether or not there is a substantive proximity between the attitude of faith and the particular notion under discussion, namely, tradition.

An additional comment should be made, namely, that tradition, once brought into the scope of the attitude of faith, ceases to be an individual quality or mode of conduct. It becomes part of the com-

---

2. Franz Joseph Molitor, *Philosophie der Geschichte oder über die Tradition* (1851). Also consult Gershom Scholem, "Revelation and Tradition as Religious Categories in Judaism," in *The Messianic Idea in Judaism and Other Essays* (New York: Schocken Books, 1971).

mon or public realm related to many individuals. We find the component of tradition in law, institutions of state, customs and modes of conduct, language, and so on. Tradition in all these domains brings into the human situation the quality of stability, inherent in the transmission from generation to generation and considered to be binding in spite of the basic fact that the transmission occurs in time. Thus, tradition becomes an interpretation of duration in spite of the continuing succession. The link between duration and succession lies in the continuity inherent in tradition.

Religions explicitly adhere to tradition because they consider themselves charged with the word of God given to human beings—not to be discarded as something antiquated but considered as something that eternally guides human response and behavior. Tradition in this sense is a synthesis of that which is transmitted factually and that which is to be a normative guide. This synthesis is essential to the realm I am here considering, and, again, an analogy to language is illuminating. Language as transmitted is of a normative character, and not only a factual one. If the normative character were not acknowledged, there would probably be no communication between human beings; that is to say, there would be no *possible* understanding between them since words as such and their syntax are the basic core of that intercommunication. There is something binding and guiding in the traditional transmission. When tradition is of this character in religion, the normative aspect is due not only to the accumulation of the process of transmission but also, and mainly, to the position of the primary documents of religion and also of faith. This is inherent in the position of the Scriptures as revelation. Revelation does not repeat itself, historically, but is present—formulated—in the given Scripture. The norms attendant to revelation are present in and through the Scriptures. The relation to them is a continuous interpretation by way of accepting them and acknowledging their normative position. But even those books that are not understood as an embodiment or an expression of a revelation—such as those expressing religious illumination—are normative because the illumination of the previous generation has the preference of being first or preceding. In any case, tradition presupposes a relation to something documentary—expressed in one way or another—pointing to the antiegocentric position of any generation that cannot ground faith in itself, or at least not only in itself. Tradition makes present the transition from the transcendent and metaphysical realm to the historical and immanent sphere, interpreting the latter as being continuously related to the focal point of the transition from the metaphysical to the human sphere. Continuity is the indication that the immanent and historical sphere cannot be independent or self-sufficient. Its dependence on transcendence has a secondary manifestation in its dependence on what is transmitted to it from preceding generations. Thus, we can say that dependence on the dimension of time, that is, the past, is itself a continuous manifestation of dependence on that which is beyond time. Tradition is a continuous process of maintaining the presence of the past by way of content and, obviously, not by way of the dimension of the past. Those who believe see themselves as sons and daughters of those who were believers in the past.

★ ★ ★

Tradition is not manifest only in the attitude to the Scriptures, although that attitude is possibly primary and determinant. Therefore, exegesis emerges as essential and thus forms the hard core of tradition. Exegesis is, by definition, related to texts; it attempts to understand them and transmit this understanding by reading the text and conveying it to subsequent generations. To be sure, as interpretation, exegesis refers to those who interpret the text or those who need that interpretation because the text proper is not open or comprehensible to them. In tradition, we find not only the relation to the past, including the texts, but also a taking-into-account of a present situation that does not have direct or immediate contact with the past. An intermediary is necessary and is implied in exegesis as interpretation.

Thus, I come to the conclusion that tradition, by its own method or possibly logic, although representing the continuous process from the past to the present and through it to the future, stops, as it were, for a while in the present moment in order to enable those dwelling in the present not only to turn their attention to the past but also to understand it and its legacy. Because of the relation to sacred texts, and probably because of the inherent nature of faith to express itself not only in attitudes and in the reading of those texts but also in conduct, tradition has absorbed an additional meaning, that of rules of moral and ritual conduct originally prescribed by the holy Scriptures which have in time attained a semi-independent status. Tradition is therefore a comprehensive process of carrying the legacy of the past to succeeding generations—while the legacy itself has a comprehensive meaning—with all that this implies of problems accompanying it, as we shall soon see.

The issue at stake is whether there exists a built-in relation between faith and tradition; religion could be considered a link between the two, and in the context of religion, we encounter a plurality: there are religions and no one religion. Therefore, there are traditions and no one tradition. Yet it can be assumed, looking into the texts, that when a certain presupposition guides tradition, that presupposition is not questioned, much less abolished in the course of that tradition.

The assumption of *Advaita* is that there is nothing but the absolute, and nothing second exists; that assumption is inherent in all the modes of interpretation and response characteristic of the tradition that starts with that assumption. Catholicism has understood itself as being characterized by antiquity and universality, and there is apparently a kind of inner relation between these two characterizations.

Yet we have to be aware of an additional structural fact, namely, that there are not only different traditions related to different religions but also traditions in different spheres of human reality or activity. We have to look into some of these modes of tradition in order to be able to highlight specific features of tradition related to faith. I have already referred to language as one of the archetypal cases of being "related" to tradition. Even when human beings are considered essentially capable of speaking, the speech at their disposal is particular and thus not a simple continuation of their basic potentiality. Speech is given to them in the process and through it. Language is conventional in its historical plurality. Yet convention, as we have noted, contains in itself normative components that enable us to distinguish, for example, between the queen's English and colloquial English. Language is in its historical expression—in its plurality—a sphere of communication and thus of human community—here again in the plural.

Let us consider another example: the institutions present in human reality that are of a historical character, that is, those established institutions that endure with or without undergoing change. Parliamentary institutions, for instance, were established within the course of history and are maintained within it, although changes related to them have occurred, such as universal enfranchisement. These changes are in many cases of a deliberate character, again, as enfranchisement illustrates. We could say, in a broad sense, that when a traditional institution fails to absorb the changes demanded of it, a farreaching reform occurs, and even a revolution. But the force of tradition tends to be so great that the revolution gives rise not to an ongoing permanent revolution but instead to a new tradition within its own province.

One of the spheres in which tradition plays a paradigmatic role is philosophy. If we speak about perennial philosophy, we may refer to the ongoing activity of philosophizing as such, but we may also refer to some issues that are present in the philosophical approach. In this sense, they are perennial issues, such as, for instance, "What is being?" "What is knowledge?" "What is the relation of knowledge to being?" or "What are the principles of human activities?" In this sense, we adhere to the tradition of philosophizing, following, for instance, the direction of Greek philosophy. Or we can discern the issues by not referring to traditional texts at all; the activity itself may lead us to discern certain issues that can be described as the ultimate data of human reflection. We can also reach the conclusion—both from the investigation of reflection as such and from the reference to basic texts—that activity proper is perennial, as are the problems. But their systematic formulation is a manifestation of perspectives. There is reflection in an abstract sense, but a perspective in a more concrete sense. If we accept the classic texts and systems not only as a focus of reference but as binding as well, we may engage in what Mandeville described as the "idolatry of human understanding." If we take Whitehead's adage about all of philosophy as but footnotes to Plato, the footnotes are not of an exegetic character but are a reflective investigation of issues that were, as a matter of fact, formulated by Plato. The first system, to put it that way, guides later philosophic reflection, not because it is given but because it has been formulated, and any reformulation cannot disregard the primary one.

An additional sphere to be considered in this context is science in the sense of the science of nature. Scientists adhere to a theory or a hypothesis, but they adhere to it not because it is given but, rather, because it stands the test of verification or falsification. The fact that the Ptolemaic hypothesis persisted for such a long period of time and thus could be considered as a basic component of the scientific outlook of the world did not turn that hypothesis into a normative theory of astronomy. Copernicus formulated a different theory, which was accepted, again, not because it was given but because it stands the test of scientific theories. There may be different relations between different theories, such as macrophysics and microphysics, but these too are prescribed not by tradition but by the criteria of verifiability.

Let me mention an additional sphere—that of art—that can be characterized in a broad sense as a nontraditional sphere. Obviously, there is a processual continuity from Aeschylus to Shakespeare, but that continuity is not one of content or approach to reality. This is so because the sphere of art, in spite of the basic structure of that sphere—namely, making media, such as words, endowed with contents—is a sphere of individual expression. This applies both to the plastic arts and to the verbal ones. Because of that basic component of art, there is no continuity in the sense of content, but there is in the sense of structure. That continuity does not refer to the past but, rather, is determined by the medium itself. In art, styles are determinant, rather than traditions.

I refer to several spheres of activities that are pertinent for the exploration of the issue before us, namely, the relation between faith and tradition as one of the links between faith, in its basic sense as attitude, and religions, in their essence as formulations of faith in concepts and norms of conduct. Religion is a historical phenomenon and has to be regarded as such. Hence, the attempt to apply the concepts of tradition, as George Hamann suggested, to the transmission of worldly wisdom is unwarranted because of the difference between history and tradition. This, in turn, leads me to restrict the applicability of the concept of tradition to human activities and not to apply that concept to the structure of the world as nature. Here again, the link between faith and religion is inherent in exegesis, which relates to something hidden. I could formulate the situation thus: the first in time is the first in essence.

This is so since faith, if it interprets itself, reaches the conclusion that the attitude inherent in it is of a basic essence and, thus, is not open to innovations because there is no need to innovate. Whatever is present in the relation to the facticity of the world and to accepting the facticity as guiding human existence, once stated, is of a permanent character. Tradition is the acknowledgment and affirmation of that basic presupposition. To maintain faith has been interpreted as patience and hope, thus underscoring faith as persistence, on the one hand, and as orientation to a longed-for future, on the other. Patience is a kind of link between the two attitudes of steadfastness and hoping. Faith is not only etymologically related to confidence. Faith implies faithfulness, and faithfulness is not an erratic sentiment but a continuous condition "without wavering" (Heb. 10:23).

It might be a viable suggestion to consider this link between faith and fidelity as a hard core of the structure of tradition as it appertains to faith and religion and also as the point of departure for turning the ancient text—from its position as a text—to its position as the guiding norm of human activities within the process and in spite of it. It goes without saying that, if the affirmation of the given implies the negation of innovation, tradition in this sense faces some problems that paradoxically become visible and even evident in the process, although the process was initially interpreted as prohibiting any reference to innovations. The idea of progress has thus to be seen as essential for the encounter between tradition and the historical process in which tradition is unable to accommodate and absorb the process.

The idea of progress is already a step beyond tradition and against it because the idea of progress implies that the future ultimately determines human activity. Therefore, expectation of the betterment of the human situation could in principle oppose the adherence to tradition. But as we have seen, since tradition is an interpretation of succession and duration, the reference to the eschatological future can be seen as part of the traditional approach in spite of the latter's obvious relation to the past.

CHAPTER ELEVEN

Bondage

This analysis has thus far focused on "faith" and "religion." I shall now try to analyze their mutual relationship, assuming that the two are not synonymous. The question as to their inner relationship remains open, namely, whether faith can be described as religion or whether it can be conceived as independent of, albeit integrated into, religion. In the terminological distinctions used in the various analyses of the issue, we see that distinctions in religion are used rather frequently. The leading one is "positive religion" versus "natural religion," where "positive" is understood negatively as something that does not emerge out of nature. Nature is understood not as a comprehensive realm but as human nature. Thus, "positive religion" as opposed to "natural religion" is considered to be posited or set. "Positive religion" seems to be synonymous with historical religions—those that emerged in the course of history and were established, to some extent, deliberately—or at least had a beginning and a specific anchor in time.

Yet even with respect to "natural religion," there are references in literature to what is called original revelation, which precedes every historical revelation and is therefore understood to be congruous with the basic approaches of human beings to the world. The distinction between "natural religion" and "positive" or "historical religions" is to a large extent similar to that between "natural law" and "historical" or "positive law."

An additional distinction should be added, that is, that between purely spiritual, noninstitutional—thus sometimes called invisible—religion, or *ecclesia spiritualis,* and religions or churches that have institutional and therefore visible form. In this context, I refer again to the basic assertion that faith can be considered a singular phenomenon since it does not necessarily lend itself to analytical and historical distinctions, whereas the concept of religion has to be seen in the plural because of the differences between approaches to transcendent reality and to the consequences that follow those approaches.

★   ★   ★

It is therefore appropriate to start the analysis of these differences, at least in their basic manifestations, by noting that faith is an individual phenomenon and that religion is a phenomenon of communal life. This difference is grounded in the fact that faith is a cognitive and reflective posture, whereas religion strictly speaking is an institution and, as such, lacks the self-awareness implied by the attitude of faith. In other words, in contrast to religion, faith is a feature of individual human existence. Religion, however, is involved in social reality and thus not confined to individual manifestations that may remain hidden or unexpressed, although, as we have seen, there are some expressions of sentiment that are indeed public. The difference between religion and religiosity is a variation of the same distinction, although religiosity obviously derives from religion. Once we maintain the difference between an individual phenomenon and a communal one, we cannot assume that there is a simple continuity from the individual to the community, and there is no simple integration of the one phenomenon into the other.

An illuminating analogue to this problematic may be found in the philosophical notion of giving an account, or *logon didonai,* which as a self-reflective act is within the province of an individual. Nonetheless, since the account is by definition formulated within terms of philosophy, it is perforce part of the system and thus has a public character. Referring to the individual character of faith, I find a formulation that is inherently an individual one, such as the notion of the God of Abraham, but when the reference is to the

God of Abraham, Isaac, and Jacob, it is already transindividual and even suggests a line of succession or a dynasty. The Hebrew term for religion, *dat* (apparently borrowed from Persian) is identical with the concept of law and thus may be understood or interpreted as implying the social or communal aspect.

* * *

The etymological origin of the term "religion," as previously noted, is controversial: the question is whether it connotes *relegere,* that is to say, "to read over again," or is related to *religare,* which connotes "to bind." The second version seems to be the more accepted interpretation, and, accordingly, I shall try to present some characteristic features of religion as a form of bondage.

Bondage can be understood as implying two interrelated directions: one is to be bound to God, and the other is to be bound to other human beings. The link between these two directions is possibly to be found in the notion of observance: maintaining a mode of conduct. The issue is precisely whether "faith" and "religion" are essentially interconnected to such an extent that without conviction there is no observance in the religious sense and, parallel to this, that without observance there is no faith. Observance has a communal character, especially once it is manifest in those modes of conduct that go by the term "worship." Worship is present in different forms of religion as honoring or revering, since religion is correlated not only to awareness but more specifically to that which is beyond the human sphere—even when that sphere is interpreted as related to human beings.

In the broader sense, observance as worship is a mode of behavior and not merely a reflective attitude. We find worship in such different forms of religion as Totemism, Judaism, and Brahmanism. Worship is closer to sacral behavior, whereas awareness cannot be conceived as containing the attribute of sacrality. An additional distinction is highlighted by that component of worship regulating what is permissible and what is prohibited. This distinction is pertinent, although one can perhaps trace its origins in "the threatening" as opposed to "the benevolent." These origins, however, cannot obscure this duality and additional ones appertaining to the determinations of behavior and their classification.

Because of the difference between awareness and bondage expressed in modes of behavior, we find in some ancient sources the difference between spontaneity and religion; that is to say, faith is spontaneous because awareness is not prescribed, while religion containing ritual prescriptions is understood to be nonspontaneous. Even the possible clash between faith and religion can be understood not as unbridgeable but as leading to a bridge or even to integration because full and lasting spontaneity cannot be seen as congruous with the potentialities of human existence.

Since religion is more formulated than faith, aspects of the difference between them may be elucidated by an exposition of the inherent structure of religion. Religions refer to God, but they emerge from the human point of view. Therefore, any human reference to God can be conceived as being analogous only (indeed, unable to overcome) the basic difference between man and God. The formulated component of religion, which, because of its communal or social dimension, is a possible ground for the institutionalization of religions. Faith cannot be institutionalized as long as it is conceived primarily as a form of cognition and individual disposition and consciousness. There is a close relation between tradition and institutionalization because tradition provides the ground and the background for stability, and institutions are stable—or at least semi-stable—by definition. Yet institutions lead to two additional manifestations. One is the hierarchy, for instance, between priest and laymen. We find that such a hierarchy is present in different religions. The other manifestation of the institutional character is the formulation of dogmas that are originally articles of fidelity and become the formulations of the direction of the particular religion. To be sure, dogmas can be seen as being on the borderline between religions and philosophy. These dogmatic or doctrinal formulations remain within the scope of religion, for they are not only guiding principles of behavior but also the content of faith. Faith proper cannot be transformed into dogmas, but once contents are corollaries of awareness, they can be conceived as belonging to faith or at least to religions in their position as presupposing faith and being grounded in it. The negative aspect of doctrinal formulations is what goes by the name of "heresy"—a phenomenon of dissent or doubt understood from the standpoint and perspective of a particular religion. Heresy is understood as a false faith or belief because it pretends to formulate its own version of the content of the religion and adherence to its teachings. Only the direction toward formulation can lead to dogmas, and only the presence of dogmas, whether explicitly formulated or not, can lead to the concept of heresy.

Since religions are modes of bondage, at least in the communal sense of that term, they look for possible means of keeping people together in their adherence and worship. Heresies are splits that endanger the bondage, at least on the level of the social community. Since religious community is intimately related to one's relation to God, it in effect contains both directions of bondage.

This institutional character of religions is further manifested in the "churches" as the custodians of religion. The task of preserving the observance—and the similarity of the roots in these two expressions is relevant—is conceived by attributing the role of trustees to the churches, constituted not only by trust in the divine entity but also by trust in the various components of the structure of the church, both organizationally and dogmatically.

★ ★ ★

I return to the point of departure of this part of the exposition, namely, that faith and religion cannot be considered identical or synonymous. From the vantage point of religion, I tried to identify components of faith which may lead to religion, although they do not necessarily do so. It is, of course, possible to conceive that relation as giving primacy to religion and from its perspective to attempt to delineate the nature of faith. The central issue seems to be that of the normative formulation of religion, since it is the other side of content. Religion aspires to present an interrelation between attitude and content, but, as happens in other areas of life as well, the content sometimes overshadows the attitude of faith.

Since attitudes are invisible and contents are open to formulation, contents become the anchor and not only the expression. I shall go on to consider a further aspect of this theme by exploring the philosophical approaches to faith and religion. These approaches are by definition grounded in reflection.

CHAPTER TWELVE

Reflective Articulation

The term "articulation" was employed frequently in the preceding chapters of this analysis. I shall now attempt to deal with articulation in a more systematic way—to "articulate articulation," so to speak. Articulation is an activity of thinking applied to the given phenomena; reflection is the other side of articulation. When I speak about a "reflective articulation," I mean a conscious approach guided by what can be described as awareness of awareness, or awareness "in the second order." I attempt to articulate or make explicit the elements of analysis of the two aspects that are our subject matter, namely, faith and religion. Yet it should be observed at the outset of this part of the exploration that there is no preestablished harmony between the reflection implied in faith and religion and the reflective attitude as second-order exposition concerned with them.

*　*　*

I shall deal with some of the most common approaches to the two phenomena without, of course, assuming to present all of the varieties of the philosophy of faith and religion or of the relation between theology and philosophy. My purpose is to outline some major approaches that recur in the course of philosophical thinking. Because of the complexity of the issue, one should note that there have been statements in the course of the development of the philosophical approach emphasizing the affinity between faith and intellect—for instance, the statement that faith seeks understanding. This implies that the shift from faith as a conscious act, an awareness, to awareness of the second order is not a leap but is grounded in the phenomenon of faith as such. But this is only one of the approaches to be found in philosophical discourse.

I shall start with the negation of the relation between faith and philosophical reflection. In negation, the paradoxical or dialectical essence of reflection gains prominence. To negate the relation between faith and philosophy, or to give exclusive preference to faith, one has to reflect on faith—in addition to one's reflection on the essence of philosophy—and present a decisive argument that philosophical reflection does not do justice to faith and even clashes with it. Because of that clash, philosophy has to be criticized or even rejected.

The negative evaluation of philosophical reflection may thus be seen as an expansion and a more detailed argument of what we find in the Epistle to the Corinthians: "God hath chosen the foolish things of the world to confound the wise" (1:27); and "Let no man deceive himself. If any man among you seemeth to be wise in this world, let him become a fool, that he may be wise" (3:18). Because the notion of "wisdom" is inherent in the term "philosophy," this dialectical process of becoming a fool in order to be wise is probably an attempt to secure faith as independent of the arguments present and essential in philosophy. Colossians (2:8) explicitly refers to philosophy, saying: "Beware lest any man spoil you through philosophy and vain deceit." These are a few of many variations on that theme, some of which I will consider as bringing out the difference and the clash between faith and wisdom or philosophy. The saying *credo quia absurdum est* (which is popularly but falsely attributed to Tertullian) is an extreme expression of this attitude: "I believe because it is absurd (that is, impossible)."

It has been asserted in some religious trends that philosophy knows nothing about God, in spite of the position of God in Greek philosophy, to which I shall refer shortly. Because of that disregard of the most overarching object of human concern, philosophy is rejected as a perverse "quest for knowledge," presupposing that knowledge is possible without divine grace. We can see this extremist statement as related to some distinctions made by Tertullian, for instance, that after Jesus we are in no need of curiosity, and after the Gospels there is no inquiry or questioning. The reference to curiosity apparently points to what has been regarded as a fountainhead of the philosophical attitude, namely, wondering. Since it is assumed that the answer to the ultimate questions of human concern has been given in Christ, there is no need for curiosity or wondering. Since an answer has been given, the question becomes obsolete or, meaningless. Hence, a distinction has been proposed between the disciples of Greece and those of Heaven in order to emphasize again the basic distinction between faith and philosophy. This distinction has a historical connotation because of the reference to Greece, but it also has a typological connotation because of the reference to Heaven.

The votaries of faith have often argued that the philosophical approach, being a false wisdom, does not affirm the distance between man and God and therefore amounts to the pretension that human beings can know the secrets of the world. In upholding the negation of philosophy and therefore of reflection, it also claimed that philosophy is not beneficial to human beings because it does not constitute a unity between cognition and deeds. Philosophy, it is held, attributes by its very nature superiority to cognition, neglecting perforce concrete deeds. This argument, perhaps, implies that philosophy corrupts man because it distracts his attention from what should be the principal focus of his concern.

*   *   *

A more moderate approach to the challenge of reflection and philosophy is represented by those theologians who maintained that there is an affinity between Platonic philosophy and faith, at the same time pointing to a duality within Platonic philosophy itself. Thus Saint Augustine, for example, speaks of the theoretical monism of Platonic philosophy and its practical polytheism. Here again, the axis is the difference between theory and practice, but this time the duality of the reflective approaches is indicated, for it does not entirely neglect the practical attitude. But should it be shown that philosophical cognition does not lead to articles of faith, one should give up philosophical cognition, preferring the knowledge of even one element of faith. Nicholas Malebranche (1638–1715), for instance, says in *De la recherche de la vérité* that a philosopher who does not teach that God does everything is a bad philosopher. This summary statement is again related to the issue of theory and practice, pointing perhaps to the position of philosophy that considers God a supreme being, but it still leaves him the object of contemplation and not a being endowed with the normative position. To be sure, historically or textually one can argue with this last statement, but this is not of concern here. I am interested, rather, in delineating characteristic approaches to negating philosophical reflection in the name of faith. Philosophy is considered insufficient for various reasons, and the identification of that insufficiency is again a reflective attitude denying philosophical reflection.

A terminological point should be made at this juncture. From what we learn from scholarly analysis, the Indian word *darsana* is considered to be the term closest to that of philosophy; it implies seeing, and from this point of view there is a kinship with seeing as implied in the Greek term *theoria*. However, there is apparently no analysis of the possible relations between *darsana* and faith, perhaps because there is no indication of a distinction between the two. Leibniz said that Chinese thinking is concerned with all the issues that are the concern of Western philosophy, including the concept of supreme being; accordingly he characterized Chinese thought as natural theology. The term "philosophy" has, of course, been incorporated in both Hebrew and Arabic and, indeed, both Hebrew and Arabic medieval religious traditions developed a lively interest in the philosophical legacy of Greece and contributed decisively to its elaboration.

★   ★   ★

Before presenting the opposite type of reflective approach, that which emphasizes the positive relation between philosophy and faith and religion, I need to comment on the term "theology."

Plato uses the term *theologia*,[1] but his term does not have the meaning of a discipline within the scope of philosophical thinking. It indicates concern with "gods," in the plural, and therefore translations of Plato do not use the term "theology" but, for instance, the "teaching of the gods." The term becomes more clearly defined in Aristotle, who deals with the relation between various modes of theoretical knowledge leading to the conclusion that there is a knowledge concerned with eternal and immovable objects that is identical with the concerns of mathematics or physics. There is a "first science," which deals with things that both exist separately and are immovable. Hence, there are for Aristotle three theoretical philosophies: mathematics, physics, and the third, which Aristotle called "theology" "since it is obvious that if the divine is present anywhere, it is present in things of that sort." This is the highest science, which must deal with the highest genus.[2] There is even a scale of the theoretical sciences, and the last one, theology, is the best, "for it deals with the highest of existing things, and each science is called better or worse by virtue of its proper object."[3] We can take it as philologically warranted that this definition or description became the basis for incorporating the term "theology" in philosophical discourse and also for discerning the positive relation between faith and religion on the one hand and philosophical reflection on the other. This will be the next point of my analysis.

★   ★   ★

According to Aristotle, theology deals with things that are both eternal and immovable. The causes operate on as much of the divine as appears to us.[4] It is clear from this statement that theology is a philosophical discipline, the highest in the scale of rationally attained knowledge. It is therefore philosophy proper and cannot be considered auxiliary to other disciplines. Philosophy does not serve theology; rather, theology is the summit of philosophy.

1. Plato, *Republic.*
2. Aristotle, *Metaphysics.*
3. Ibid.
4. Ibid.

It is obvious that the characterization of philosophy as *ancilla theologiae*, which became part of the vocabulary of the twelfth century, ascribes a secondary position to philosophy, both in terms of the concept, applied and referring to the theological reservoir of ideas and concepts, and also in the sense of presenting possible arguments for the sake of the basic convictions present in religion and therefore made explicit in theology.

As long as philosophy is considered as providing explications of concepts in the various religious traditions, the notion of philosophy as *ancilla theologiae* could be adjusted to given conceptions of faith and philosophy, respectively. But philosophy presents not only precise concepts but also arguments—and here one may question whether arguments of the sort used in philosophy can be discerned in a faith grounded in Scripture. To be sure, there are some, at least terminological, conjunctions between philosophy and faith like *philo-christus* or the attempt to bring together the philosophical eros with a love of God. But philosophical arguments in support of faith call for a new approach that probably cannot be incorporated in what we have already discussed.

★   ★   ★

Arguments are justifications of statements; therefore they are proffered as proofs. In modern philosophy, there has been some mitigation of the notion of proofs, using as an equivalent or surrogate what Max Scheler (1874–1928) described as pointing (*Aufweis*) or pointing after (*Nachweis*). However, some major trends of philosophical discourse, mainly in the Middle Ages, were concerned with demonstrations, that is, with formulating arguments for traditional religious concepts, mainly of the creation of the world and the existence of God. Maimonides (1135–1204) claimed that there is (that is, could be) no philosophical argument denying the creation of the world.[5] Therefore the biblical account can be accepted. If there were a philosophical argument against creation, "the gates of commentary would not be closed." Thus,

5. Maimonides, *Guide to the Perplexed*, chap. 63.

the superiority of the biblical account is implied. The validity of the philosophical argument hovers somehow on the horizon as a nonverified possibility. The biblical account remains authentic since it has not been invalidated by philosophical argument.

In the concept of creation, as it has been explored in philosophical discourse, we find again a combination of articulation and demonstration. In Philo, for instance, we find a reference to God, his power and will as the ground of nature and time. These are already explicit statements that can be conceived as transposing the biblical narrative into conceptual explications like the will of God, the relation between time and space, and so forth. The biblical narrative does not refer to creation out of nothingness; rather, it refers to the chaos that precedes the order or the cosmos established by the act or event of creation. Inasmuch as the total sovereignty of God became dominant in the philosophical discussions of creation, the aspect of nothingness became important because it is considered a correlate of the absolute sovereignty of God, which would be diminished by any reality coeval with and independent of him. This is an argument that brings not a total novelty to the discourse but emphasizes that which can be understood as being present in the Scripture, and calling only for articulation.

From a typological perspective, I can now introduce "gradations" in the hierarchy of reality. In reality, there are different levels—for instance, body, soul, earth, and heaven. Where we identify levels of reality, it is necessary, as Saint Anselm argued, that there should be one level that is not related in its facticity to other levels. The presupposition seems to be that reality cannot be conceived as an infinite or indefinite structure of levels. It has to have a beginning, and that beginning is not only a beginning in time but also a beginning of a distinctive and necessary mode of reality. A restatement of that argument is the difference between possibilities and necessity. Where there are possibilities, they too cannot be indefinite. They have to have a basis in what is beyond them and thus conceptually, in what is a necessity, differing from the other levels of reality in being self-sustained and thus capable of positing the other levels. Recourse to such arguments is probably based on a presupposition that God is not conceived as immediately present in human awareness and cognition. One needs not only an exploration—which is still a matter of making concepts precise—but a conclusion, and that can be attained only by employing arguments at least as instruments in order to reach the desired conclusion. In a way, the conclusion is present in the Scriptures, although it is formulated not as a conclusion but as a statement.

This argument, referring to the structure of nature or the universe, in terms of plurality and unity or possibility and necessity, can be considered a restatement of Aristotle's position on theology. Aristotle's position was made more explicit in the specific arguments formulated in medieval philosophy, such as the argument of "first cause" or "first mover." The negation of an indefinite series of causes is inherent in the different formulations of that argument.

Referring to the structure of the universe, an additional nuance becomes significant in the formulation of the argument; the focus of the argument is the structure of the universe not in terms of levels of reality but in terms of order. As a matter of fact, in this context we find transformations or restatements of the metaphor that, just as a ship does not move of its own momentum but needs navigating, so the regular course of events of nature needs the act of setting in motion or at least that of guiding by a suprahuman and supranatural being. In this argument, we find a kind of analogy between the artificial structure of a human instrument and its dependence on a navigator and the lawful structure of the world. This analogy emphasizes the fact that many of the arguments are actually based on the observance of encountered reality and lead to statements related to suprahuman reality. As is well known, this argument in favor of God as architect was considered by Kant as the only viable or semiviable argument after he criticized and rejected the other arguments, which he called the cosmological and ontological proofs for the existence of God.

The cosmological argument or proof is essentially a restatement of Aristotle's position, while the ontological argument can be considered an extreme articulation of the inherent unity between thinking and reality implied by the concept of God; reality is considered one of the manifestations of the supreme being. In the variations on the theme of these arguments, we find explicit or implicit reference to Aristotle's presentation of theology as the highest level of philosophical thinking, incorporating some of the fundamental notions relevant to theology as the basic philosophical discipline. Theology ceases to be in the service of philosophy. It actually becomes identical with it, and the conceptual formulation already present in theology in the traditional sense becomes self-established in theology as a philosophical discipline. We arrive here at the notion that philosophy and theology are identical because, philosophically speaking, the *theos* is the highest reality and thus corresponds to the fundamental position of theistic belief. The Neoplatonic theory of emanation was absorbed into some of the philosophical trends, probably because of the accepted structure of the universe as a hierarchy starting with one, out of which the plurality of the world emanates.

★ ★ ★

Before considering what is perhaps the most extreme formulation of the conciliation and even identification of religion and philosophy—Hegel's system—I shall comment on one trend in the religious approach that has been articulated in philosophical terms, namely, mysticism. Mysticism is considered to be the elevation of the soul. Since mysticism in some of its trends aspires to the highest possible union of the human soul with the one being, it can be considered a variation of the theme of *homoioisis*—becoming similar to God—whether or not that stage is eventually arrived at. In this sense, mysticism starts with the gap between man and God but considers human capacity and human aspirations as potentially capable of going beyond these factual limitations and reaching the highest possible stage in the relations between man and God. Again, many of the mystical thinkers assumed that the soul possesses an inherent potentiality for a unity or unification with God. Hence, some of them transposed philosophical concepts to the sphere of mysticism. This is so even when the basic difference between cognition and *unia mystica* is maintained, though the love of God common to both philosophy and belief can be considered a bridge between the two.

Hegel can be considered the most extreme of the philosophers in his dialectical conflation of religion and philosophy, in spite of his well-known objection to philosophy as edifying. He probably thought that once the identity between the two realms was accepted, philosophy would cease to be edifying because it would become a conceptual reformulation of religion, insofar as philosophy is the cognition of reality aiming at identity with it and eventually arriving at it. Philosophy ceases to be only the love of the highest level of cognition but becomes that level itself. This indeed is related to the view that philosophy is a science of the absolute—the absolute, not as it was hitherto understood as being separated from reality, but as the comprehensive being and, thus, including in itself all the essential components of reality.

As Kant noted, art and philosophy are expressions of the same content, though in art the expression is in images or representations, while in philosophy it is in concepts or ideas. In a way, Hegel considered religion to be a popular philosophy, presenting its content in representations and not in ideas. There is a difference in terms of adequacy between religions, as well as between art and philosophy, but their basic content is the same. Hence, to know reality and to be identified with it amount to the final goal of knowing God. Again, God is considered here not as a separated transcendent reality but as one identical with total reality as adequately understood. Nevertheless, Hegel uses the concept of God and even says that philosophy is the perennial service of God—and one could ask whether this statement, clearly a metaphor, implies an edificatory intent in spite of Hegel's programmatic statement against philosophy as edification. In any case, since spirit is immersed in immanent development, it becomes identical, step by step, with absolute reality in its development; that identity is expressed in art and religion and eventually formulated in philosophy. I shall return later to Hegel's position, taking a critical stand, with the view to restating my thesis that faith is a sui generis phenomenon.

★   ★   ★

I began this discussion by considering some negative evaluations of philosophy, and I may end by referring to the negative evaluation of philosophy insofar as it is conceived as being identical with religion and, thus, related to the negative evaluation of religion. I refer here to Ludwig Feuerbach (1775–1833). According to this disciple of Hegel, philosophy has to emancipate itself from its self-deception, which is the other side of the mésalliance between itself and theology. Philosophy has to become again a matter of human concern, or—to put it differently and negatively—theology has to be dissolved in anthropology. Anthropology must be conceived in its own boundaries and not engage in pseudoaspirations of going beyond or above them. Hence, there is no need for a conciliation between religion and philosophy since philosophy is to be seen as an independent activity and one that is entirely adequate to comprehend human existence. We should mention here that, for Kierkegaard, human existence becomes a point of departure for a leap to God and thus does not allow for what Hegel regarded as an immanent, albeit dialectical, union with the Absolute, or God.

The most extreme anthropological interpretation leading to the negation of faith and religion is the attempt to apply the notion of "fetishism" to both phenomena. The notion of fetishism was initially applied to characterize primitive magical beliefs, emphasizing that what people believe is actually made—*facere*—by human beings. Essentially, fetishism has been understood as a kind of idolatry with the significant reservation that idols are not symbols of entities but are entities in themselves. In the process of applying the notion of fetishism to religions, it ceased to be a restricted characterization of primitive religions and was extended to characterize manifestations of "stupid reverence," or as the projections of human beings' wishes and expectations in general. As a fetishistic phenomenon, animated by a projection of wishes, religion was deemed a grand fiction.

At this point, one may mention that Kant uses the term "fetish" or "fetish making" in the context of sorcery or superstition, thus retaining the original meaning of the concept. But there is a second connotation in Kant's analysis, namely "fetish-worship," which he interpreted as being identical with the rule of the clergy or of the church constitution, which provides for the dominant position of the clergy. In this context Kant introduced the difference between moral laws and statutory rules. One could say that the introduction of the notion of fetish into that context is a negation of religion as an external, statutory order. This far-reaching criticism of religion is a negative corollary of the extreme moral interpretation of faith or even of religion, if the latter is understood within the ethical context. The rejection of idolatry is in this sense also far-reaching because it leads to a distinction between religion in its essence and its external manifestations that are beyond moral intentions and take on institutional structures. In any case, the tension in the original meaning of "fetishism" is a manifestation of that attitude of philosophical criticism which leads to the negation of faith in the religious sense. "Fetishism" is understood as pointing to what is artificially contrived or to what is supposed to be endowed with independent power but is essentially an image of man and not that of an independent entity.

Looking now at the term "hypostasis," with which fetish was often identified, it should be observed that that term underwent extensive transformation in the course of philosophical thinking and the development of philosophical terminology. "Hypostasis" was originally one of the terms synonymous with "substance." In Christian theology, we find at least one of the versions of that term as referring to the union of the divine essence and human nature incarnated in Christ. Yet, in the course of time, "hypostasis" ceased to characterize an independent substance of the underlying layer of reality and became a term for what is falsely regarded as substance. The self-subsistent reality became a fictitious reality. Once the term is applied to the sphere of faith and religion, it indicates the interpretation—and this is present in Kant—that the object of faith and religion in its full reality is a mere representation. As Kant said, it is first realized and eventually made into an object, then hypostasized and finally personified. This too, precisely because of the transformation of the term, is one of the expressions of the negative evaluations of at least of some of the concepts of theistic faith and religion.

Nietzsche absorbed these critical evaluations of religion and took them to their extreme. According to him, God is not just a projection of human beings; he is the opposition to life and its enemy. Projection implies despair vis-à-vis human existence. It is immoral to believe in God. For the sake of the affirmation of life, "God has to die and the superman has to live; the free spirits will be freed."[6] The traditional interpretation of man as an "image of God" turns man into an "ape of God." Nietzsche's negation of religion is possibly the most extreme, while his affirmation of the human being is correspondingly the most radical.

Having presented some of the basic approaches to the relation between faith and religion on the one hand and philosophy on the other, we may return to the systematic problem: In what sense can faith be considered a phenomenon sui generis, and what may be the task of philosophy in exploring that phenomenon? This again will require a systematic analysis. I shall begin with a comment on what can be regarded as the phenomenology of religious consciousness.

6. Karl Löwith, *Von Hegel bis Nietzsche* (Zurich and New York: Europa Verlag, 1941), contains instructive analyses of the conceptions dealt with in the last part of this exploration.

CHAPTER THIRTEEN

The Core

Having discussed various conceptions of the relation between faith and religion, I return to the beginning of this analysis, where I try to identify the essence of faith, taking into account that I am dealing with a phenomenon that has been interpreted in various ways and, because of its relation to religion, has taken different historical shapes. When the range of historical manifestations is so vast, the question of whether the essence can be identified is of central importance. Still, I try to characterize its essence—as far as is possible—by separating the phenomenon of faith from its various historical and empirical manifestations. Furthermore, such an identification may possibly enable us *post factum* to see that the historical manifestations, though not identical with faith in its essence, are still related to it.

I shall try to formulate what may be described as a phenomenological approach to faith: to identify some inherent features of faith, taking as a point of departure the assumption that there are such features. They can be taken as calling either for adherence or negation, yet they have to be seen as features of a phenomenon, not as related basically to a weltanschauung.

Before continuing this tentative approach, I shall make some comparisons with other phenomena that have both essential and historical features. The most obvious is language because its many variations have a historical character. Nevertheless, we can isolate the essential core of languages, the synthesis of sounds and meanings. That synthesis is an underlying one, empirically present only in sounds where those sounds are variegated in spoken or historical languages. One could add that sounds are replaced in the written manifestations of languages by characters that maintain the meanings and are again a synthesis either of sounds or of visible characters. A synthesis is present also in the sphere of knowledge that, broadly speaking, is an identification of states of affairs guided by the principle that the identification has to present an adequate report about the state of affairs. That principle is the principle of truth. In this sphere, we can accept the basic synthesis as characteristic of it, although, as we know, truth can be interpreted differently because the question remains open as to whether the state of affairs referred to can be isolated, taken in its fragmentary manifestation, or has to be seen in a certain context. The context is open to characterization concerning its scope and the relations among the particular state of affairs and the inescapable context. One could say that one of the differences between everyday and scientific knowledge is related to the issue of the connection between the state of affairs and the context. Theories or hypotheses are tools or structures asserting contexts. The move from the principle in the sphere of knowledge to spheres guided by principles like that of ethics is an open issue.

To start this phenomenological exposition, I refer to Rudolph Otto's notion of holiness. One could interpret Otto's conception as a phenomenology of the consciousness of faith and religion, starting with the correlation between that consciousness and its objective pole, characterized as holiness. To be sure, the reference to the notion of holiness gives priority to the objective pole because the entity related to is holy while consciousness is not. Yet consciousness responds to holiness, and that response has some essential qualities. Otto understands the holy as tremendous, numinous—that is to say, essentially characterized by qualities beyond the human position and consciousness. The qualities as such evoke the attitude of being fascinated, and so forth. One could argue that Otto's analysis is a phenomenological one because he refers, as said before, to the correlation between consciousness and the noematic pole without assuming a possible distinction between the ontological component of the holy and holiness as such.

One could further argue that, once the point of departure lies in consciousness as given, there is no room for the distinction between the ontological and the sacral component. As the correlate of consciousness, the two components are integrated.

* * *

Yet the question of the ontological core, the relation to which is characteristic of faith, cannot be eliminated, because faith, even when understood as an attitude of response, is essentially based on the affirmation of the superiority of the extrahuman dimension. It is faith as conjecture or assertion because the ontological element is not given. Nevertheless, it is considered essential for human awareness, including human response. The ontological element is referred to by human awareness, but at the same time it is understood by it as being "beyond," not only spatially but even more so by the impossibility of knowing it. Faith is an awareness, self-aware of its limits, which cannot be overcome. I shall now consider some aspects of this in-between position of faith.

* * *

It seems plausible to focus the consciousness of faith on the notion of holiness. There could, however, be some historical doubts on the matter—that is, whether holiness is central in various modes of faith or whether it is a kind of expansion of what is inherent in theistic religions.

The first question to be raised is not of a historical character but a structural one, namely whether holiness is considered the last or independent notion upon which all other notions within the scope of the consciousness of faith must depend. Holiness is basically a concept connoting sublimity, which is meant to evoke reverence or imitation of its inherent norms within the human sphere. Can a concept attributed to the divine entity be a predicate, or does it have to be a subject? Conceptually speaking, I am asking whether we can remain within the normative dimension only, or whether we must have recourse to the ontological one. The sublimity of the divine entity is not only of a normative character, or of an ethical impact, but is also to be seen as ontologically grounded. The same question, although differently formulated, applies to human consciousness as such, that is, whether it can be considered basically fascinated by the sublime entity or whether there is bound to be more of a symmetry between that entity and human consciousness as it responds to it.

We should consider the possibility that the essence of the entity evoking human response is the totality of the world as it is present, although its presentness can never occur within the limited awareness of any human being. Human beings encounter parts of factual reality. They refer to the total factual reality by being aware that what is given to them in their limited scope of existence and awareness cannot be identical with facticity proper. "Facticity" is synonymous with "totality" but not with the totality of any of the manifestations of human creativity, such as numbers or languages. It is the totality of that which is real. It is a universal sphere, never directly encountered. I postulate that there is such a sphere. I do not assume that the total sphere underlies that which is phenomenally given, like the concept of the thing-in-itself, nor do I assume that the totality is of a paradigmatic character, like the idea in Plato's sense. It is factual and yet not given. The notion of creation is an attempt to understand or explain the facticity of this basic facticity and is thus an additional step toward that which is phenomenally encountered, bringing into the context an act or event with a causal connotation. That which is factual and thus not explainable is made into the object of an explanation that is not based in facticity but introduces the correlation between cause and effect, with which we are conceptually acquainted in the sphere of ordinary human cognition.

★ ★ ★

The ontological component that is central in the context of faith as conjecture is reinforced by the component of eternity—a topic I have already considered. At this juncture I can say that eternity can be attributed to facticity because the total sphere is not open to change as such; it is only parts of the sphere of facticity that change, which in the course of changing do not introduce change in the position of the total sphere. There may be a difference in terms of the precise meaning of eternity, whether it is attributed to facticity or is brought into the context of the divine entity creating the facticity. At this juncture, it is appropriate to refer to one of the descriptions of eternity, *nunc stans,* which refers to the ongoing presence of eternity within time and not beyond time. This characterization has also been formulated as "now without time" or "as everything within the now." These descriptions are closer to the sphere of facticity than to that of the divine entity outside facticity even in the universal sense. To be sure, in some of the philosophical characterizations of the divine entity, that entity was described as "standing now," and that description went with that of being unique, simple, and so on. Yet these characterizations apply also to facticity in the universal sense because, by definition, that facticity is unique: there can be no two *total* facticities, though perhaps it might be difficult to characterize that totality as simple. The common link between the totality of the factual universe and the divine entity is that both are transcendent. The question remains, What is the point of departure for situating transcendence? In other words, Is it a universe in itself or the sum total of what is at least potentially open to human encounter?

One could say that we have here two possible interpretations of transcendence: one that could be described in historical terms as pantheistic, and the other as theistic. With respect to faith as conjecture, there is perhaps no way to decide between these two possibilities because to a very large extent they are grounded in the same view of the universe as beholden to a transcendent God. Both refer to transcendence—the pantheistic interpretation refers to transcendence as encompassing the world, while the theistic interpretation refers to transcendence as utterly separated from the world and self-contained. Yet by introducing these two interpretations of transcendence, I offer the possibility of enlarging our understanding of the various modes of faith, including those that are essentially nontheistic. From this point of view, polytheism can be considered as polytranscendence, with all the attendant conceptual difficulties of seeking to maintain transcendence together with plurality.

Returning to the notion of holiness, I repeat that the ontological basis, whatever its interpretation, is present both in universal awareness and in awareness directed toward universality; similarly it is the presupposition for interpreting the transcendent entity as holy. This is significant because transcending the limitations of human awareness as far as possible—and there is controversy on this issue in philosophical thinking—is apparently the first step from the perspective of human awareness in the direction prescribed by the attitude of faith. If that which is the object of faith is that which is totally different, then that description applies to transcendence in the sense of the universe as well as in the sense of the divine entity. Furthermore, while emphasizing the position of that which is totally different, I avoid to some extent the temptation to attribute to that dimension some predicates that we are acquainted with from human experience, such as overwhelming power, total sovereignty, and so on. These characterizations are derived from human experiences or encounters with various spheres of activities, including relations between individuals or the impact of institutions on everyday activities as well as on more permanent modes of behavior. If I assign a unique position to the noematic aspect of the object of faith, it follows, to some extent analytically, that the possibility of applying attributes from the human sphere to it is denied. If faith is a conjecture, it has to retain this essential quality, and thus it does not learn, as it were, from human experience (that is, in its interhuman dimension), although it still constantly refers to the broadest contours of reality or facticity.

It is noteworthy that it was precisely those philosophical interpreters who tried to bring the meeting between philosophy and faith or religion into context who were aware of the conjectural character of religious awareness. It is not by chance that they used descriptions like *docta ignorantia,* which for them connoted a religious consciousness grounded in a certainty but not an argument. They also used expressions like enigmatic science (*scientia aenigmatica*). Applying these descriptions, they attempted to formulate the character of the attitude of faith notwithstanding the various parallel attempts to express the neomatic aspect of faith conceptually.

* * *

A plausible argument could be made concerning the affinity between faith as referring to transcendence and metaphysics in the philosophical sense. Still, the difference between the two spheres is inherent in what has already been said since there is a basic difference between conjecture and argument. An argument refers to a procedure, while a conjecture is a leap. Both start with human awareness and lead that awareness to its possible peak or final point. Yet in a sense metaphysics, once it reaches that point, comes back to the beginning, attempting to present a synoptic view of the possible links between the various strata of reality. If faith does not present an affirmation based on argument, it is not obliged to show links between the different spheres or the procedure from the ultimate facticity as transcendent to that which is immanent. This is so even when the notion of creation is employed because creation is a situation, condition, or event arrived at by conjecture in the face of the arguments employed in the various philosophical expositions.

Faith is awareness and, by the same token, also self-awareness. Even those who refer to the illumination in faith cannot be oblivious to the corollary aspect: namely, that by referring to the ultimate stratum of reality, we are referring to something that may illuminate reality and yet, at the same time, lacks explanation. There is no need to elaborate on this because, for if the presence of the divine entity is an amenable explanation, then it would not be the ultimate datum. The same applies to the ultimate position of universal facticity; in this sense, the pantheistic explanation, claiming to be of a geometric mode, cannot explain the very presence of the universe. The most it can do is explain its structure, and here too, as Spinoza's systems indicate, the explanation is confined by human perspective to two attributes only—cognition and expansion.

One could argue that arriving at the ultimate stratum of facticity is not unrelated to human awareness, which transcends consciousness here and now, or that it is related to what Husserl called the external horizon. He described that horizon as comprising what he called "objects-with" (*Mitobjekten*). We could say that the horizon is not confined to objects that are with us at least potentially. It is the totality of objects. Yet I do not point to that horizon without being aware of the self-transcendence that may lead us to what is considered the ultimate horizon and as such is asserted or affirmed by awareness as conjecture—conjecture because we, by definition, never meet the ultimate horizon and move only within it. The step taken toward the ultimate may be well grounded, but it is still a conjecture. This aspect leads me to an additional consideration of the human response to that which is conjecturally affirmed, namely, expectation. Here, too, I distinguish between the core and its manifestations. Therefore I cannot take fascination or even reverence as the corollary of consciousness to that which is noematically affirmed. This will be the next part of my exposition.

★ ★ ★

Expectation, too, presupposes awareness. The latter is an attitude of cognizance, while the former is an attitude of anticipation. It presupposes awareness also in the sense that the total facticity is not only the horizon of cognizance but also the horizon of that which may occur and is expected to occur. Expectation goes beyond the present moment and is reinforced by awareness since the latter opens the horizon for that which is expected. From the point of view of faith, and of religious faith in the more specific sense, expectation can be characterized as an attitude, indeed, a posture of faith that confidently awaits the realization of what is awaited. Faith ascribes the realization of the anticipated event or development to the influence of the transcendent realm. Again, without cognizance, expectation is impossible, though it goes beyond cognizance. Expectation refers to the possible response of the transcendent reality and thus becomes the focus of religious faith in the stricter sense of that term. While awareness can be confined to the reality encountered, faith, though grounded in the awareness of reality, brings into its scope the expectation of being granted something by God—even if there are differences of opinion or of faith as to what precisely is to be granted. One of the possible interpretations entails the conception that facticity as such is already granted—through the act of creation, for instance—and thus openness is not only one of the horizons but also the horizon of forthcoming divine responses to human faith and expectation.

⋆　⋆　⋆

To be sure, expectation is not confined to the sphere of faith or religion. It is part and parcel of everyday human reality that goes beyond the immediate moment and thus is intentionally directed toward what is about to come. Here expectation presupposes not only awareness but also the dimension of time, time as succession and not as duration—the aspect I discussed previously in the context of tradition. The presupposition of time as succession amounts to the presupposition of the ongoing character of reality. That character does not necessarily mean the indefinite continuation of that process. We can expect something since there is something beyond the instantaneous moment and what is contained in it. Whether what we expect is repentance or redemption, whether it is to be encountered in the scope of personal reality or in the scope of the historical process—all these are possible interpretations of the posture of expectation. Since this posture cannot be separated from awareness, we keep returning to one possible meaning of Peter Abelard's (1079–1142) statement that nothing can be believed that has not already been cognized. Even when we do not speak of a theistic interpretation of expectation—focusing, for instance, on the Buddhist faith in redemption from the cycle of existence through the abolition of human suffering—expectation is central. The end of suffering is anticipated by way of what can be described as negative redemption, or redemption that is contrary to affirmation of reality. In other modes of faith, like the Second Coming of the Messiah, the aspect of expectation is obviously central. To be sure, these are significant differences in terms of the interpretation of reality, that is to say, whether reality is to be affirmed or overcome.

★   ★   ★

The conjunction between awareness and expectation that is essential to faith can be viewed from another point of view. Facticity in its totality, and certainly in its connotation as transcendence, may have two meanings; the first is totality as such, and in this sense totality can be that which is facticity and that which is beyond facticity, in other words, the creator. The second meaning is those parts of facticity that become present within the scope of the encountered reality, and when considered as belonging to something beyond themselves, those parts may be taken as granted by the act of creation. Here again there are several possible interpretations. The most extreme would be the occasionalist one, according to which everything that is present becomes so by the act of intervention by the divine entity. There is a more mitigated version of this position, namely, that the divine entity created the factual world and gave it its own momentum, including its own structure. But an even more mitigated interpretation faces problems such as universal providence or particular providence, that is to say, whether the creator intervenes in reality or not.

For the sake of a broader overview, we should note that a religion may occasionally adopt a fatalism. Therefore the question of the very possibility of expectation emerges at this juncture: Is expectation just a human fallacy, or does it have some grounding in the structure of reality as an open, dynamic process? It is appropriate to adduce the adage that everything is seen and freedom of choice is given, in order to point to a kind of ambivalence or paradoxical oscillation in certain aspects of faith that attempt to maintain both the openness of reality and its dependence on the transcendent structure or the creator. Here again, the openness of reality that includes the possibility of a nonillusionary human expectation can be understood as a response to the goodness that is one of the renderings of facticity's open structure. The potentiality of being good both in character and through deeds is understood by several interpretations of faith as associating human beings with the goodness of the transcendent reality. The goodness of that reality, through its presence within the immanent reality, brings the dimension of goodness into the scope of human reality. Once we consider goodness to be connected to aspirations, we also consider it to be linked with expectations. Thus expectation as a feature of the relation between human existence and faith is again emphasized. I could further define this feature by pointing to two components of this expression of faith: expectation in general, which goes beyond the immediate moment but is neutral in terms of its direction, and expectation directed toward specific goals or acts that are benevolent and thus are good thematically, which is more than merely presupposing the potentiality toward goodness.

★ ★ ★

Faith is structured not only by the nature of human consciousness but also by the objective structure of the phenomenal world or concrete reality. Awareness of the facticity of the world amounts to an awareness that reality is encountered and not created by human beings. In encountering, human beings encounter the limitations of their own existence. The question they face is whether the awareness of their limitations should serve as an impulse for their urge to stretch the limitations as far as possible, or whether it is a kind of perennial reminder that there is no escape from those limitations and that it is even mandatory or obligatory to maintain appropriate standards of restraint as an ongoing norm of human conduct. Faith, because it also prescribes an order for human conduct, is anchored in that awareness of those limitations by turning the awareness into a prescription. Here again the prescription is not totally alien to the basic awareness of human beings but amounts rather to an emphasis of its governing direction. It is significant to mention this not only in the context of human behavior or norms in general, but also—and mainly—against the climate of opinion of technological civilization that may lead to the view or illusion that there is no limitation to the human urge to dominate reality and that eventually reality opens the possibility for what can be called "cosmic imperialism."

Faith in its various manifestations may be a focus for a reformulation of human self-awareness as it encounters facticity and learns to appreciate the resulting limitations of human action. These possible transitions from discernment to norms do not presuppose a simple continuity between the two. They suggest, however, the possibility of finding a bridge between different approaches to the question of faith and religion from the perspective of human awareness. A banal comment may be permissible here. Faith and religion are human perspectives, even when they refer to transcendent reality or to the divine entity. A human perspective is prominent in several components of both faith and religion, including that of the relation between awareness and conduct and the link between those latter two components that to some extent lies within the realm of expectation and norms.

Awareness is the presupposition of the various modes and directions pertinent to the exploration of the phenomenon of faith. It underlies the other cognate phenomena, including as noted, expectation. Awareness is not confined to any one of these phenomena, and it is expressed in all modes of orientation of those presupposing—actively and not only conceptually—a specific orientation. Thus awareness underlies knowledge in the more methodical sense of that term, as it underlies expectation with its particular characteristic features. Awareness can be as passive as reception or, at least, can be considered as referring to accidental impressions or to the mere presence of a human being in his surroundings. The active component of awareness increases when it grants special attention to specific matters, and here again knowledge is a case in point. Indeed, awareness of facticity as the comprehensive realm is already, at least partially, similar to the direction of knowledge because it is a deliberate step beyond the fleeting impression, and it is focused on an object that can be described at least verbally. But unlike knowledge, awareness of facticity, by definition, goes beyond the context of a given object and directs its intentionality toward that which is the comprehensive sphere of all contexts or is the context at large that again cannot be cognitively comprehended in its structure because of its transcendent—that is, comprehensive—character.

* * *

As awareness underlies expectation, so expectation underlies confidence, which is an additional component of the attitude of faith. Hence, I can say that we encounter with confidence an ascendance in terms of activity; that is, the more focused awareness becomes, the more active it is, and thus a confident reaching beyond that which is given increases by way of the activity on the one hand and the specific focus on the other. Confidence is animated by the expectation that what is expected will, indeed, come to pass. Confidence is not confined to intentionality toward the broadest facticity or to transcendence. It amounts to a focused expectation since it is identical with a sort of hope that the expectation will be met or fulfilled. There can even be a relation between confidence and trust in interhuman relations and personality, and not only to the discrete acts of the persons involved, since confidence is not a fragmentary act but presupposes a trust in the person to whom one extends one's confidence and directs one's activities. Hence, there can be a relation between response and responsibility. Confidence is thus directed toward a response because it presupposes a responding and responsible person, thus implying a relation between constancy and response.

These aspects of confidence are, of course, present within the general human situation. They are also present in faith in the more specific sense applied to the sphere of belief and intentionality toward transcendence. These elements of faith become prominent in the sphere of religious belief in the expectation of divine care and providence but also in the expectation of forbearance or forgiveness. The mutuality characteristic of confidence in general is present also within the scope of faith when human beings express thankfulness to God as a ritualized formula of gratitude not only for God's past but future deeds. Thus faith posits a correlation between reverence on the part of human beings and response on the part of the transcendent being or entity. Because of these components, confidence in general and in the sphere of faith specifically bestows a sense of security on human beings. The relation between faith and confidence is thus not only etymological but also thematic. Because of the human component of confidence, one person may trust that another or many others will equally respond to transcendence as he or she does. Even self-confidence can be important in this setting because human beings entertaining faith are confident that they do not err or deceive themselves, in spite of the lack of empirical guarantee for their belief. Yet in terms of correlation or mutuality, faith as confidence can be seen as a strictly human phenomenon since human beings are meant to be confident, whereas this attitude does not apply to the transcendent being. The step taken from faith as an attitude to religion as a set system of norms and beliefs can be understood here when one notes that one of the features of religion is a totalization of confidence. Religion is meant to evoke confidence, and I return to the relation previously indicated between awareness and sentiments.

Religion is meant to evoke conviction, presupposing the relation between confidence and conviction. Even when despair is taken into account, faith and religion are meant to overcome despair by evoking hope and eventually leading to a situation, which at least in terms of one's mood, will induce confidence and thus mitigating despair.

At this point I underscore the relation between confidence and respect, though respect bears the connotation that the respected object or idea is sublime and as such we cannot grasp its essence. Because of these features, conjecture is an aspect of faith. Nevertheless, confidence, though related to reverence, does not exclude the affirmation inherent in confidence but, on the contrary, is meant to lead to it. Sublimity connotes here not only that which cannot be grasped but also that which will meet the highest possible human expectations. This position possibly implies a view or a conjecture that, within the human scope, the sensuous component of human reality renders a permanent response of confidence impossible, whereas with the relation to transcendent reality, where there are no sensuous inhibitions, confidence does not face the obstacles present in the human sphere. It is because of that implied assertion that faith carries with itself an optimistic direction that is applicable even to those of its manifestations that deny the validity of terrestrial reality. The very assertion that the overcoming of urges and passions is possible is a manifestation of confidence and thus eventually contains an optimistic interpretation that is expressed, in this case, not in the affirmation of given reality but in its negation. Here again, I emphasize that the meeting between faith in transcendence and faith in goodness and its realization is, in this sense, not accidental.

*   *   *

In the above analysis of the defining features of faith, I have referred to the direction of faith toward reality, although awareness is not confined to that direction. Awareness is, however, self-awareness, or at least can be so. Hence a further step in the attempt to explore the essence of faith leads me to the aspect of self-awareness present in faith. Faith is self-certainty; it is a certainty that is justified and grounded in its own scope and cannot be nullified. I do not mean to say that there are no human beings who reach the conclusion that their faith is false and renounce it. But insofar as faith is a constant attitude, it contains in itself the self-assurance as to its constant certainty. In a way, faith knows itself because its certainty is self-certainty; it is not intrinsically open as knowledge is to falsibility or refutation. In contrast to faith, knowledge is self-scrutinizing and self-correcting. Faith, being aware of itself, does not scrutinize itself. It is self-contained and thus may reach the conclusion, right or wrong, that it must persist despite conflicting evidence or experience. Here I can ask the structural or phenomenological question, Why is it that faith as a phenomenon of awareness seeks to sustain itself, as indeed it does in spite of much evidence that might undermine it? One explanation of this feature of faith is that, since it is by its intentionality directed toward transcendence, no empirical occurrence is entitled to weaken it. Once faith ignores or dismisses empirical data, or once human self-transcendence is meant to be corroborated by the realm of transcendence, the relation is not one of evidence but one of conjecture. In this sense, a conjecture seems to be more stable than a hypothesis in the sphere of knowledge because it is by definition a conjecture and therefore self-contained, or at least can be so interpreted. This does not mean that one entertains faith because it is an absurd. It means that the empirical criteria are not pertinent to faith, if at all, when expectation is its most salient feature. Faith in its core is a certainty that is not warranted by knowledge or empirical data. One can say reflectively that human beings need faith in order to maintain faith. These and similar aspects of faith are prominent in positions or attitudes even such as agnosticism or atheism, which I shall now consider.

CHAPTER FOURTEEN

Exposition and Identification

The approach underlying this analysis has been phenomenological. Some qualification of the term "phenomenological" is necessary. I am not using it to refer to a school with a defined teaching or doctrine. I am interested in a broad orientation in order to indicate that my analysis refers to the phenomenon of faith and attempts to describe its essence, taking historical manifestations into account and trying to find a possible, though limited, synthesis between the historical and the essential, or at least a relation between the two.

Since I am speaking about phenomenology, I should mention Max Scheler's presentations of what he considered to be a phenomenological analysis of faith.[1] Faith is a synthesis of a conception of the divine reality and a valuation of the highest good.[2] Faith negates the possibility of finding for itself a ground or justification, but it is nevertheless endowed with evidence.[3] It is an essential part of every finite consciousness.[4] Yet Scheler was apparently not satisfied with these conclusions and tried to find a connection between faith and what he called feelings of sympathy. He could make this attempt since he characterized love as the most prominent feeling of sympathy.[5] This attempt to identify faith as essen-

1. Max Scheler, "Möglichkeiten der Realsetzung der Gottesidee und die Idee der Selbstmitteilung," in *Schriften aus dem Nachlass*, vol. 1, *Zur Ethik und Erkenntnislehre* (Bern: Francke Verlag, 1957), p. 182.

2. Ibid., p. 184.

3. Scheler, "Glauben als Aktart," ibid., p. 244.

4. Ibid., p. 245.

5. Scheler, "Über Scham und Schamgefuhl," ibid., p. 118.

tially love calls for some critical observations precisely because that emphasis turns out to identify reverence as a secondary aspect of faith. Thus Scheler regards religious devotion as a variation on general attitudes and emotions of sympathy, including love. One can, however, argue that reverence is at least as central to faith as love. Islam, for instance, is very emphatic in stressing the self-dedication of man to God, more so than love. I mention this because it is necessary to consider the variations of faith when we attempt to determine its essence and to delineate the systematic possibility of arriving from this essence to its variations. Hence, the centrality of awareness seems to be justified not only from the phenomenological point of view but also from the perspective of a possible shift from essence to its historical manifestations.

★ ★ ★

Scheler's emphasis on feelings of sympathy seems to be a variation of Pascal's *Raison de coeur*. Here, too, I have to question whether dichotomies such as those that are implied in Pascal's view can do justice to the various aspects I am concerned with or whether the neutrality of awareness, and its relation to facticity as such, can serve as a more proper point of departure for the analysis that may do justice to the phenomenon of faith.

The meeting between faith and philosophy has taken different shapes, some of which I have already analyzed. I should reemphasize what I shall now call the instrumental aspect of philosophical concepts—those concepts brought into contact with notions inherited from beliefs, "traditions," or "religions." When Plato calls God *demiurgos,* he does not use that term arbitrarily since he is pointing to divinities acknowledged in the framework of a state.[6] The most significant step taken philosophically in bringing systematic concepts together with the traditional notion of God is Aristotle's employment of the term *energeia.* Traditionally, in mythological orientations, God is understood as might. The concept of *energeia* implies activity in the first place: the overcoming of

---

6. *Demiurgos:* see Plato, *Republic* 529d; *Timaios* 28a.

obstacles. As actuality, it connotes the constancy of activity. Aristotle uses this term for the description or definition of the notion of God that he obviously took, not from his own systematic vocabulary, but from a source external to his own work, attempting to incorporate the notion into his system. If *energeia* connotes constant activity, it is beyond the conjunction between matter and form and can be understood as form only and, thus, as a telos of the reality composed of matter and form. The purity of form is epitomized in the concept of *energeia*. It thus becomes the cause par excellence and can be employed by the attempts in the later philosophical systems that try to point to the ontological position of God and concurrently to his impact as the cause. The concept of *energeia* implied holiness as a possible aspect of God, but as such it gave priority and therefore also supremacy to the ontological status of God, which is the precondition or presupposition of the axiological status of holiness. As a transformation of Aristotle's system—for example, in medieval philosophical systems—a kind of a coming back to faith and religion occurs: Aristotle transferred the concept of God to the structure of his system, whereas medieval philosophers applied Aristotle's concept of God to that expressed in religious texts or attitudes. It goes without saying that those philosophers tended to understand *energeia* as synonymous with *dynamis*, and not with *potentia*. The Aristotelian tradition can therefore be regarded as an attempt to bring together as complementary philosophy and concepts deriving from religion, and not as an attempt to identify or amalgamate philosophy and religion.

★ ★ ★

It is in this context that I shall now return to the systematic position of Hegel's view of religion, specifically as related to what he deemed to be the fundamental affinity between religion and philosophy. I shall deal here with Hegel's position in some detail since it can be taken as formulating a view that a phenomenological approach cannot accept. For Hegel, faith is the relation of finite beings to the Absolute.[7] He tries, however, to show that the polarity between the infinite and the finite cannot be accepted as an ultimate characteristic of the structure of reality. Philosophy, according to Hegel, cannot accept the view that the finite is *only related* to the infinite.[8] If faith is interpreted in this sense, it can only be an initial reflection.[9] Faith in the religious sense, he maintains, attempts to give expression to the Absolute[10] and thus faith is grounded in the spirit, in which the Absolute also shares.[11] Faith as such does not contain the awareness that it is thinking.[12] Thus the explication of faith through thinking is not an application of extraneous concepts to the finite consciousness but is a step toward the sublation of faith toward the infinite.

There is a distinction between the real spirit and that which the spirit knows of itself.[13] Because of that distinction, religion, even a revealed religion, precedes philosophy in time since only philosophy is the spirit's true cognition of itself,[14] and on such issues it is also chronologically a "latecomer." Religion contains in itself the true idea of God or the Absolute, but it does not reach the level of the adequate relation between the concept and the idea and that which is the content of that idea. Religion is truth for all human beings.[15] The emphasis laid on all human beings indicates that religion has something of a popular character, and, thus, it is in religion that a people gives definition to what it holds to be true.[16] Because of religion's character in its relation to a people, it stands inherently in the closest relation with the principle of the state.[17] The difference between philosophy and religion is only that of the

---

7. Hegel, *Aufsätze aus den kritschen Journal der Philosophie*, in *Werke*, ed. Glockner, 7:57. All unascribed citations are to Hegel and refer to the Glockner edition.

8. Ibid., p. 293.

9. *Grundlinien der Philosophie des Rechts*, 7:229.

10. *Vorlesungen über die Philosophie der Religion*, II, 15:161.

11. Ibid., p. 229.

12. *Vorlesungen über die Geschichte der Philosophie*, III, 19:546.

13. *Phänomenologie des Geistes*, 2:524.

14. Ibid., p. 614.

15. *System der Philosophie*, III, 10:459.

16. *Vorlesungen über die Philosophie der Geschichte*, 2:84.

17. Ibid., p. 85.

mode of the latter.[18] In this context, Hegel emphasizes the old hostility between religion and philosophy. That hostility is probably due to the tendency of a particular stage of consciousness and history to maintain itself without the inner realization that it is only a transitional stage toward the ultimate stage inherent in philosophy. When Hegel speaks in traditional philosophical terms in dealing with religion, he is actually attempting to convey that philosophy will sublate the images of religious presentations to concepts and ideas. This is so since philosophy is concerned both with the concept and the content, thus implying the move from the finite content to the absolute and infinite one.[20] Religion as the mediation of the finite spirit is related to finitude, and thus it is the cognition of the divine spirit from the perspective of finitude.[21] In religion, human beings look for the ground of their dependence, and they find tranquillity in having the infinite before them.[22] Essentially, religion has thus to be felt, and unless it is within the realm of feeling it is not truly religion.[23]

★   ★   ★

Absolute knowledge is the ultimate shape of the spirit[24] and, as such, is expressed in philosophy. That which is "in itself" becomes "for itself,"[25] or, to put it differently, that which is is has to be conceptually conceived. This is the task of philosophy because that which is is amenable to reason and thus also to conceptual articulation.[26] Philosophy is the thinking idea.[27] Philosophy makes itself explicit when it explicates religion, and in doing so, religion explicates itself.[28] Thus religion needs philosophy because philosophy is eventually the adequate manifestation of that which is im-

---

18. *Vorlesungen über die Philosophie der Religion*, 2:38.
19. Ibid., p. 51.   21. Ibid., p. 216.
20. Ibid., p. 177.   22. Ibid., p. 330.
23. *Vorlesungen über die Philosophie der Religion*, II 16:385.
24. *Phänomenologie des Geistes*, 2:610.
25. Ibid., p. 613.
26. *Grundlinien der Philosophie des Rechts*, 7:35.
27. *System der Philosophie*, III, 10:474.
28. *Vorlesungen über die Philosophie der Religion*, 15:37.

plied in religion. Religion receives its justification in philosophy.[29] The unity of thinking and being that is the basic idea of philosophy is implied in religion, but it is not conceived as such. The Christian religion represents the absolute essence, but it does not conceive it conceptually. Ultimately, philosophy does not do anything but articulate the idea of Christianity in rational concepts.[30] Religion is, in fact, a plurality of religions; that is to say, the various religions have to be seen in the process of leading toward self-conception step-by-step or stage-by-stage, though that self-conception remains within the scope of religions as one of representations (*Vorstellungen*) as opposed to conceptual articulation. Philosophy, too, is a process of philosophies, leading to the self-conception of reality as reason. The basic affinity between religion and philosophy is one of implicit character, whereby the explication of the truth of religion proper becomes the essence and the task of philosophy.

Underlying this basic affinity or even identity between religion and philosophy, as already indicated, is the notion of reason. Reason confirms all reality as being. Self-consciousness and being are one and the same essence.[31] As the confirmation of all reality as being, reason elevates reality to truth.[32] Reason is the highest unification of consciousness and self-consciousness or of the knowledge of an object and the knowledge of itself.[33] Philosophy is the science of reason. Reason unifies the various alleged contradictions,[34] including the contradiction between the finite and the infinite. Philosophy does not deal with religion as a self-contained sphere but as one imbued with reason before reason became explicit and aware of itself. This interpretation of the basic relation between philosophy and religion, which led Hegel to conflate the two realms, is probably grounded not only in the interpretation of reason but also in the interpretation of Christianity as a religious

29. Ibid., II, 16:353.
30. *Vorlesungen über die Geschichte der Philosophie*, III, 19:8.
31. *Phänonemologie des Geistes*, 2:185–86.
32. Ibid., p. 335.
33. *Philosophishche Propadeutik*, 3:111.
34. *Aufsätze aus dem kritischen Journal der Philosophie*, 1:60.

phenomenon. As a historical phenomenon, it points, Hegel held, to the essential structure of religion, which is not only historical. As a bridge between Hegel's systematic consideration of religion and the reference to Christianity, the position he assigned to mysticism must be taken into account. Mysticism, he argued, is something mysterious only to the understanding (*Verstand*). Since it implies the concrete unity between human consciousness and the Absolute, it is akin to reason (*Vernunft*), and not to understanding. In mysticism, God is conceived as present in the subjective consciousness, and that unity expressed in what Hegel calls the *Ausbildung* of Christianity.[35] The mystery is something, which beyond conceptualization, is essentially speculative and, as such, is deemed by Hegel to be ultimately amenable to reason. Again, everything that is speculative is inconceivable to understanding and, as such, is a mystery.[36]

★ ★ ★

Hegel's exposition of the concepts essential for religious faith is imbued with the notions of his system. Reason underlies the system, and the self-knowledge of reason is the goal of the system and its ultimate explication. Hence, the analysis of particular concepts characteristic of faith is meant to lead to the concretization of the system. These concepts are abstracted from the whole setting of religion and, therefore, at least as a matter of principle, can be analyzed as Hegel does. The question remains whether such a method, which might be warranted with respect to the explication of particular concepts, can be applied to the broad scope of religion as a historical phenomenon, as, for instance, Christianity. I shall now look into some of the characteristics of Christianity as Hegel formulated them.

Hegel says that only Christianity gave, in the doctrine of God becoming human, a completely free relation to the infinite, and concurrently in the doctrine of the presence of the Holy Spirit in the community of faith. Those doctrines, he argued, allowed for

---

35. *Vorlesungen über die Aesthetik*, I, 12:49.
36. *Vorlesungen über die Philosophie der Religion*, II, 16:532.

the conceiving cognition of the spirit in its absolute infinity.[37] In this programmatic formulation, it is noteworthy that Hegel speaks about God becoming a human being, and not about God becoming Christ. Thus he gives a universal meaning to the incarnation that may be consistent with the universalization of spirit in his system, but one may wonder whether it does justice to the teaching of Christianity. Moreover, the notion of the absolute spirit that is different from that of the individual or particular spirit[38] does not necessarily lead to the universalization of God becoming human. The motive behind Hegel's formulation of the essence of Christianity becomes apparent when he says that the new religion made the world of philosophy intelligible to the world of common consciousness.[39] Even when we accept the affinity between the religious conception and the philosophical one, that affinity does not blur the distinction in terms of the fundamental difference between Christ and every human being. When Logos becomes flesh, that particular and singular event does not connect the Logos with the individuality of the human individual as such.[40]

Hegel had to come to grips with the position of cult in a historical religion; in his view, cult is the relation of the finite spirit to the Absolute. It is because of this, Hegel adds, that we have the component of cult in all the elements of religion before us.[41] Yet there is bound to be a difference of the spiritual or intellectual relation of the finite to the Absolute and the relation to the Absolute inherent in cult since cult is the sum total of acts expressed in a ceremonial conduct. Thus cult cannot be considered identical with knowing God as Spirit, even when it is assumed that it helps to achieve that goal. The conception that man has an absolute infinite value does not lead to the conclusion that man and God, or the objective and the subjective idea, are one.[42]

Hegel's interpretation of the death of Christ as bringing the fini-

<hr>

37. *System der Philosophie*, III, 10:10.
38. *Vorlesungen über die Aesthetik*, I, 12:120.
39. *Vorlesungen über die Geschichte der Philosophie*, III, 19:104.
40. Ibid., p. 102.
41. *Vorlesungen über die Philosophie der Religion*, II, 16:223.
42. *Vorlesungen über die Geschichte der Philosophie*, I, 17:190.

tude of human beings to the true consciousness of the Spirit[43] all but ignores the particular circumstances of Christ's death. It is not so much that Christ gave up his individuality[44] but that he was subject to death by an act of humans. Hence the identity of divine and human nature did not become conscious in an immediate way in Christ, because the finite existence of Christ is understood as divine incarnation and cannot be conceived as immediately present in human consciousness.[45]

★   ★   ★

I have noted these aspects in Hegel's interpretation in order to highlight the basic issue, namely, whether or not a philosophical approach to faith must necessarily lead to an interpretation of the components of faith as inherently part of a harmonious system. Accordingly, we also question whether or not Hegel's conception should eventually be formulated in the articulation of the conceptual components of faith and religion without losing the inner perspective of the phenomenon itself, even when articulated by the philosophical reflection. This question may also be addressed to art and science and to other spheres of activity considered by Hegel, which can be conceptually analyzed without being integrated into a harmonious system and which, as such, may be questionable. It becomes even more questionable when it leads to an oversystematization of the historical phenomena that are brought into it by "paying the price" of being denied their particular essence.

This overharmonization is particularly striking in Hegel's interpretation of such a central element or concept in Christianity as grace. Hegel says that divine grace demonstrates the basic fact that human nature is not truly alien to divine nature.[46] Grace is the spirit of God in man. Hegel seems to have been oblivious to some of the central statements of the Epistles to the Corinthians, for ex-

43. *Vorlesungen über die Philosophie der Religion*, II, 16:305.
44. *Vorlesungen über die Geschichte der Philosophie*, II, 19:119.
45. Ibid., III, 19:132.
46. *Philosophische Propadeutik*, 3:98.

ample, We receive not the grace of God in vain (2 Cor. 6:1): By the grace of God I am what I am (1 Cor. 15:110). There can be no interpretation corresponding to the text that can give these formulations the meaning of a basic identity between humans and God. God becoming human is a particular event or act and not a manifestation of a hidden essence. It is because of this that Saint Augustine interpreted grace as a free gift—*gratia gratis data*. A gift is grounded in an act coming from the outside, and thus grace emphasizes the distance between humans and God, not their identity.

It is appropriate to mention that Hegel discusses amnesty in the context of his legal philosophy as the right to grant forgiveness,[47] and calls the right to grant amnesty one of the highest acknowledgments of the majesty of the spirit. This is so because amnesty amounts to the power to undo that which has been done or to nullify a crime by forgiving it. Hegel thus overemphasizes the possible ontological impact and meaning of the act of amnesty, for to forgive is not to nullify that which has been committed. It is to renounce the response or reaction represented in punishment by the society or the sovereign of the state. Nothing that has been done can cease to be part of reality. Hegel overinterpreted amnesty because of the systematic trend of his thought to bring the finite existence and infinity close together, in this case by suggesting that the finite response becomes part of the past, but not only this—his understanding of it amounts to turning existence into that which does not exist. The infinite sphere must absorb into itself all the possible manifestations of the finite.

A critical examination of Hegel's conception may be guided by discerning two approaches: (1) his attempt to interpret the historical phenomenon of religion, albeit mainly of Christianity, and (2) the basic presupposition of his interpretation of religion as inherent in his concept of a philosophical system. When there is a clash between a particular historical manifestation and his systematic philosophical approach, Hegel invariably says, So much the worse for the facts.

★   ★   ★

47. *Grundlinien der Philosophie des Rechts*, 7:392.

A secondary issue will bring out this difficulty of Hegel's system, namely, his analysis of fanaticism. Fanaticism, he argues, is a passion related to understanding and not to reason. Hegel examines fanaticism within the context of Indian religious belief as well of Islam and Judaism. From this historical perspective, he claims that fanaticism basically destroys that which is concrete, that is, the faith or belief of other human beings.[48] Even the alleged stiffneckedness of the Jews is understood within the context of fanaticism.[49] Hegel does not deal, at least not in detail, with the shift from religious to political fanaticism and does not analyze the etymological and thus possibly thematic relation between fanaticism and *fanum*, which connotes "temple." Therefore, he does not see fanaticism as one of the manifestations of the overconviction characteristic of faith, where certainty grounded in arguments is lacking. To some extent fanaticism is a pseudocompensation for that lack. In addition, fanaticism, though expressing passions, is in many cases a component of cult since the fanatic's convictions remain often within its orbit. Interestingly, Hegel does not analyze the transition from convictions to acts in his presentation of the essence of religion.

I return to the proposition that it is the task of a philosophical study of the phenomena of faith and religion to give them a conceptual rendering. Contrary to Hegel's presupposition, such a conceptual articulation does not lead to the establishment of a harmonious system. Various spheres may coexist in a system and even clash. For Hegel, such a view was—pragmatically—only an external reflection. But reflection is bound to be external. By its very nature, reflection enables a variety of spheres to be maintained without being reduced to one particular sphere even when that one is philosophy. Paradoxically or dialectically, elevation is also a reduction.

I am concerned with Hegel's conception of faith and religion because in it components of faith and religion are both analyzed and placed in a philosophical system based on transitions from

48. *Vorlesungen über die Philosophie der Geschichte*, 2:16.
49. *Vorlesungen über die Philosophie der Religion*, II, 16:85.

one sphere to another and ultimately on the convergence of all spheres in the philosophical system. Hegel's conception of the system is based not on the coexistence of spheres but on their replacement by a higher sphere and eventually by allegedly the highest one, that is, philosophy. He did not consider faith or religion in their own terms. He saw the constant features of any of the spheres from the perspective of the systematic position of philosophy as the synthesis of all spheres of life and of all the predicates attributed to them.

★   ★   ★

At this point, then, it is methodologically appropriate to add some comments on a significant attempt to view faith from the point of view of its own meaning and structure and to consider it as the highest manifestation of humans' relation to the world. The advocates of this approach contend that the vision of faith and not its conceptual structure is salient, and not as a synthesis but as a coincidence or, in Cusanus's terminology, *coincidentia oppositorum*.[50]

In speaking of vision, one must recall the place of vision in the Scriptures and in what Xenophanes says about the eye looking on the whole heaven and the statement that God is one. In the Bible, the reference is to Moses, who spoke to the Lord face to face (Exod. 33:11), to seeing God face to face (Gen. 32:30), and "I will come to visions and revelations of the Lord" (2 Cor. 12:11), though 2 Corinthians 5:7 we read: "For we walk by faith, not by sight." Probably the use of the metaphor of seeing—and one must acknowledge the metaphor—is intended to emphasize the direct encounter between humans and God, though Maimonides says that only Moses encountered God in this direct way. In addition, another metaphor, that of light, has a bearing on the introduction

50. On the difference between Hegel's systems and the vision of Cusanus, see Werner Beierwalte, *Visio Facialis—Sehen ins Angesicht: Zur Coincidenz des endlichen und unendlichen Blicks bei Cusanus*, Bayerische Akademie der Wissenschaften Philosophische-Historische Klasse, Sitzungsberichte, Jahrgang 1988, Heft 1 (Munich, 1988). Beierwalte rightly juxtaposes the two systems—that of Cusanus and that of Hegel—though his formulation of the difference between them differs from that presented in this chapter.

of the notion of seeing into the context of faith;in other words, since human beings are enlightened by revelation, they see it, or they even see God revealing himself. Illumination is introduced into the human scope, and seeing is a human response to the light that does not eliminate the enigmatic character of the encounter. Yet seeing or vision are also present in Plato's theory of ideas, and the notion or term *theoria* contains the root of seeing. I suggest that the introduction of the notion of seeing into the philosophical context and the context of faith emphasizes not only the immediate character of the encounter but also, and more particularly, the fact that the ultimate stage of seeing closes the door for arguments, or second thoughts and revision, or even for continuing discourse. Seeing denotes the end of the discourse.

In mysticism, however, which can be described as a philosophical interpretation of faith, seeing is not only a vision but also a union between the seer and what he sees, and even more so when his own seeing is a manifestation of that which is seen. Since that which is seen is opposed to that which remains hidden, or that which is hidden becomes revealed to human beings in their mystical union—and here it should be noted that the Greek term *aletheia* amounts to becoming manifest—I can say in summary that the process of being enlightened allows the interpretation that light evokes vision, and vision is essentially a union.

It is rather difficult to argue with the presentation of vision because it is largely of a testimonial character, precisely by not being argumentative. I shall soon deal with the argumentative aspect implied in the notion of the coincidence of opposites. Is it possible to maintain the position of a unity between humans, however enlightened, and transcendent being? It may be possible to maintain the unity in terms of the essence of the transcendent being because essence is of a qualitative character, but, in the ontological sense, the position of transcendence is not open to a unity if transcendence is to be maintained. We cannot have it both ways, insisting on transcendence and proposing the path toward unity with transcendence. The unity blurs the fundamental distinction between the immanent and the transcendent. In this sense, the seeing eye, with all the attraction inherent in that notion and its description, is probably not the most appropriate image for the encounter between human beings within their own sphere and transcendence in its sphere. The emphasis on the supraintellectual or suprarational aspect or essence of the mystical encounter cannot blur the difference between that which is within its scope and that which is beyond it.

Though there is a relation between coincidence and vision, I distinguish between these two components or trends and seek to show the difference between coincidence and synthesis. Coincidence stresses the fact that different predicates coexist; synthesis stresses the fact that the different predicates form a structure with built-in interrelations. Thus it carries the meaning of a harmony—and, indeed, this is the presupposition governing Hegel's system. But if faith is only partial knowledge; it cannot know everything, including the harmonious structure of the essence of the transcendent entity. Here the affinity between faith and conjecture again becomes important, and thus conjecture (let us not forget that Cusanus used that term) cannot be interpreted from the point of view of the medium or the instrument of vision. This observation leads me to the conclusion that faith is not only a phenomenon sui generis but must also be conceived as occupying the borderline between itself and reason and its structure. That borderline cannot be overcome by any structure grounded in transitions and synthesis.

★   ★   ★

From this observation I come to the additional conclusion that faith cannot be identified, in Kierkegaard's sense, with the absurd. Kierkegaard saw the absurd as the object of faith and, indeed, as the only object permitting faith. He identified the object of faith with the absolute and, strangely enough, tried to establish a symmetry between the absolute relation on the part of the individual and the absolute as the object of his faith. But one must question whether the absolute can occupy a position beyond that of the ultimate horizon as transcendence and can be identified not only with that which is beyond intelligibility but also with that which is absurd—that is, that which defies intelligibility. Pari passu, one must question whether the relation to the object of faith is, indeed, an absolute, that is to say, totally separated from other attitudes, and a phenomenon that is not only sui generis but also utterly isolated from other human attitudes. The antithetic character of that statement, pointing to Hegel's synthesis along with Kierkegaard's antithesis, becomes evident here. It seems better not to conceptualize faith. Conjecture is an awareness of human beings who may attempt to comprehend the transcendent entity, being aware of their cognitive limitations due to their finitude and because of the unique position of transcendence. If God is so great that there is no end to his greatness, or if God is the magnitude in totality and there is no limit to that magnitude, then not only is synthesis impossible, but vision is also impossible because it would go beyond the limitations inherent in faith as such and its position within the human scope.

To return to mystical vision, I must say that, because of its character, it cannot be separated from the human experience, even if it is considered its summit. Again, granting the testimonial character of its presentations, day-to-day existence is not overcome, the corporeal dimension of that existence is continuously present, and so also is awareness of the finitude of human existence. From a structural perspective, a conceptual interpretation of faith has the advantage that is experientially and methodologically separated from experience. By being conceptualized, however, it can be depersonalized; nonetheless, we may question whether faith can be depersonalized and still remain faith. Again, to have it both ways, to maintain the essence of faith and to separate it from the context of human experience, is questionable. To be sure, one may question that questioning because of the testimonial character of mystical statements.

CHAPTER FIFTEEN

Negation and Restrained Affirmation

This survey of various conceptual approaches to faith and religion may be supplemented by a reference to two negative approaches, agnosticism and atheism. Programmatically, agnosticism is a conception emphasizing that knowledge is bound to be one of the empirical or natural sciences. Thus knowledge refers to data and to establishing or constructing their functional interrelations. From the point of view of the empirical or natural sciences, there is no justification for overstepping the boundaries of science in an attempt to affirm a transcendent reality. This is the essence of the agnostic position, whereas calling faith or religion an "abomination" goes beyond the structural confinement to science as the paradigm of knowledge. We can look at agnosticism in light of the astronomer Pierre de Laplace's (1749–1827) well-known remark that he did not need the theistic hypothesis to explain the heavens observed by his telescopes. What Laplace offered was in effect an elaboration of Kant's criticism of dogmatism and the cosmogonic proof of the existence of God. An overriding skepticism thus informs agnosticism.

Yet one has to distinguish between lack of knowledge and denying by way of argument the claims of knowledge about the transcendent realm of entity. The position of knowledge as dealing with functional relations of empirical data does not provide grounds for affirming transcendence. But neither does it deny the affirmation from the point of view of faith as differing from knowledge and concurrently does not deny the position of transcendence as such. The contradiction is between agnosticism and what is called "creationism," and not between reliance either on science or on faith. Creationism does not allow for immanent functional relations between data or occurrences and tries to establish, as it were, a scientific position introducing into the scope of immanent occurrences the continuing intervention of the creator in the very existence of particular occurrences or entities. Creationism is not even satisfied with the narrative in the Book of Genesis that says that man was created by a particular act. It considers creation to be a persistent continuous intervention of God in the concrete world. Hence agnosticism should be regarded as essentially opposed to creationism and may still leave the way open for faith, though the position of agnosticism as such does not lead to faith. As long as faith is accompanied by self-awareness that it is faith and thus conjecture and not empirical knowledge, there is a duality and not a clash between faith and knowledge. This should be stressed as a matter of principle, though faith is not always accompanied by that self-awareness, which serves as a restraint, whereas science is more germane to the position of self-reflection and thus to self-restraint. Hence reflection on science need not necessarily reflect faith.

★   ★   ★

Atheism differs from agnosticism because, as the term implies, it basically denies the position and perforce also the impact of the transcendent being. The distinction between the transcendent realm and the transcendent being or entity must be stressed in an analysis of atheism. If we take, for instance, Nietzsche's conception, we cannot be oblivious of his—expressed and implicit—interpretation of transcendence. Nietzsche deals with the world at large and therefore with eternity or eternal recurrence. He relates human existence to the *fatum*; he does not limit himself to affirming the factual status of fate but tries to evoke a particular positive attitude to it. He therefore focuses on the conception of *amor fati*. *Amor* is not only an affirmation but also, to use an expression derived from the philosophy of religion, an ascent. Reference and positive relation to fate are meant to give human existence a position within the universe in the overwhelming sense of that term. Thus the relation to transcendence is present in Nietzsche's conception of *amor fati*. When he says that God is dead, he implies that God has been alive and his death is his disappearance from the human sphere. That disappearance is not identical with the disappearance of the realm of transcendence. To be sure, transcendence has to be understood here as the most comprehensive sphere of the world as it unfolds. That sphere is not only a framework of occurrence but, through the attitude of loving, *amor fati*, turns out to be of focal significance for human behavior and expectations.

Yet we can understand atheism not only as a negation of the divine entity but as negation of the whole transcendent realm, based on the argument that within immanent reality there is no ground for establishing a transcendent one. From the position of faith, however, one can argue that transcendence and its affirmation are based not on an argument but on an interpretation of facticity that is not identical with particular events, occurrences, or entities encountered within the sphere of immanence. Thus, I return to the characterization of faith as conjecture, and from this point of view the question arises whether faith can be accompanied by its self-awareness as conjecture and can maintain itself within the limits of that attitude.

Self-reflection would not change the essence of faith, though it might be understood as a philosophical addition to the discernment of the essence of faith. Hegel characterized atheism as a conception that takes the finite as absolute. Obviously, this characterization introduces distinctions imbued with systematic connotations, as the terms "finite" and "absolute" indicate. Criticizing atheism, I can say that the reference to the transcendent realm is grounded in a phenomenological analysis characteristic of that which is given rather than in the reference to a transcendent entity. Perhaps the two references can even be distinguished from each other. Their common feature is the overstepping of the empirical data, and this, of course, is a constant of the attitude of faith.

★   ★   ★

I conclude this part of the analysis by quoting two maxims by Goethe: "Only the constancy of phenomena is significant; what we think about this is a matter of complete indifference."[1] The maxim is formulated in general terms, but it can be applied to the phenomena of faith and religion. Historically speaking, these are to a very large extent constant phenomena, even indifferent to cognitive elaboration, whatever its direction. This constancy, and its corollary indifference, can be viewed as expressing the difference between conjecture and knowledge. It can also be understood historically in the sense that faith and religion are a kind of popular metaphysics grounded not only in historical phenomena but also in the inclination or disposition of human beings in general to be concerned with metaphysics.

A second maxim of Goethe's is also appropriate in this context: "An active skepticism, which attempts always to overcome itself in order to reach knowledge governed by laws, is a condition of trustworthiness (or faithfulness)."[2] Obviously, an attitude of active skepticism is more germane to knowledge than to faith, which can be seen as inherently negating skepticism. Nevertheless, there is a possible connection between reflection scrutinizing itself and an active skepticism as on overriding attitude. When faith presents itself as endowed with a certainty that cannot be questioned, it runs counter to the attitude of active skepticism. From this perspective, there is a primacy of thinking and reflection even when that primacy does not lead to the consequence of its alleged supremacy. Once an attempt is made to maintain both faith and an active skeptical attitude, that attempt is grounded in the last resort in the understanding that faith, including religion, is a human attitude although its focus is beyond the human realm. The supremacy of the transcendent reality as viewed in faith cannot erase the primacy of the *noesis* manifest in faith.

* * *

1. Goethe, *Maximen und Reflexionen.*
2. Ibid.

The central point of my analysis is the sui generis character of faith as an attitude implying certain concepts and components. When we come to explore the meaning of that broad statement, we are bound to be involved in a paradoxical situation, namely that we cannot escape using concepts and descriptions applied to the phenomenon of faith from "the outside." The very fact that we employ the term "attitude" is already an indication of that paradox or dilemma. The etymological root of attitude is related to being fit for something, and one may wonder, to say the least, whether faith can be related to the situation of being fit for something.

Still, we may ask whether the specific, irreducible character of faith can be at least partially explained. The attempt should be made in terms of presenting some components of this concept. One is the depth of the attitude of faith—and here I come back to the testimonies or expressions formulated by persons of faith, as in the Psalm: "From the depths I called to you." The person of faith is aware of the depth of his faith, which takes precedence over all the partial aspects important in dealing with human behavior or positions. The depth cannot be expressed by any possible articulation once it points to the roots of the attitude, by way of a sort of symmetry: breadth and depth. Awareness of the gap between the depth of faith and any expression accompanies all attempts to render the essence of faith conceptually; it is bound to accompany it.

The conjunction of depth and breadth has dialectical consequences. One of them is the possible and, indeed, the actual profession of faith that it is all-comprehensive, that it contains in itself all possible encounters with the world, including those implied in various disciplines such as astronomy, physics, biology, not to mention those such as history that are concerned with human actions. Yet a fundamental difference exists between the orientations of the various disciplines and the orientation of faith: scientific disciplines including those in the humanities, such as history, attempt to explain detailed phenomena or events by connecting events among themselves. Faith is not an explanation of events, not even of the fact that there are events at all to which the various disciplines refer. Faith is an attitude of grounding and not of ex-

planation. The historical clash between that attitude and the hypothetical explanations is manifest in the history of religions. That
clash may be taken as an indication of a built-in difference between
grounding, relying on the consciousness of certainty, and various
theories and hypotheses intended to provide explanations. As an
act of grounding or drawing from the depths, faith is self-
interpretative as well as comprehensive and, as such, contains all
possible, let alone actual, approaches to the world. However, there
is still a clash here that cannot be explained away.

The trend toward comprehensiveness, and concurrently a further expression of it, perforce begets an acknowledgment, often a
begrudging and negative one, of multiple religious faiths. It is perhaps not an accident that religions are originally not tolerant of
one another. Tolerance is by and large an attitude or approach
guided by social and cultural trends that are beyond religion and
have an impact on religions, if at all, post factum. The depth,
breadth, and certainty implied in faith cannot be proved and thus
cannot be disproved either. These elements inherent in faith contain the trend toward self-containment and consequently nontol-
erance. Intrinsically, religious views see themselves as exclusive
and monopolistic, though in the course of history they are bound
to face the plurality of religions and acknowledge it at least de
facto, with the gap remaining between a de facto encounter and
the de jure acknowledgment. Metaphysical reflection is, however,
bound to overcome any skeptical attitude, though it may be accompanied by it, at least in terms of the awareness that any formulation of reflection referring to totality is necessarily only partial.
The reflection on totality may try to come to grips with the continuous process of reality and continuing interpretations of it. Totality can be understood as a focus of reflection, but any formulation
of it is bound to be partial. Plurality of expression of the reflection
on totality is also bound to be present in any synoptic reflection,
not only because of the historical consciousness accompanying
philosophical reflection but also because of the awareness—reflection on reflection—of the gap between the focus and its formulation.

These comments lead us to a further observation again related to the built-in paradox or dialectic of faith. Faith is a human attitude directed to the suprahuman dimension or reality. That direction seems to be understood as granting a transhuman dimension, not only to the noematic pole of faith, but also to faith as such. The certainty that faith contains as essential to its very nature is the transposition of the total self-sufficiency of the transhuman position to its human interpretation. Faith here encounters the dilemma of, on the one hand, being certain because of the *noema* it refers to and, on the other hand, being human and therefore directing itself in terms of the *noesis* to the transhuman dimension. Some of these dilemmas become prominent in various expressions of faith, including that of theodicy. The question is how to be certain and still to wonder—and thus to look for a way to present a formulation of that dilemma. The attitude of science as expressed in the attitude of trial and error is the other side of the awareness that any theory is hypothetical and thus only provisional. Since faith is an attitude of grounding in the dimension of the Absolute, it may, and does, ascribe absoluteness to itself. Here again, the absoluteness of the *noema* is perhaps ascribed in a secondary way to faith as referring to the Absolute. Religions, inasmuch as they formulate codes of belief and behavior, regard themselves as expressing this certainty of faith.

The aspect of awareness, as I have stressed time and again, is inherent in faith. I must add that that aspect is not merely awareness as such. It cannot be detached from acts or deeds if we understand the latter as the component of intervention in the surrounding world. The initial conjunction of awareness and acts is one of the prominent qualities of faith. Here again, we cannot escape the question whether that conjunction can be explained. By way of comparison, I say first that the direction of what is meant by the notion of *ataraxia* does not seem to be congruous with faith, since tranquillity of the soul may be conceived as a blessing granted to the soul but not as an immanent goal achieved, for instance, by refraining from taking a stand in the face of events. The affinity between *ataraxia* and apathy cannot be overlooked when we try to understand the essence of faith. Apathy cannot be considered essential or primary in the context of faith once the relation to the transpersonal realm is by definition a component of faith and essential to it even when, as in Vedanta, the person is not active. He is still an observer—*sakschin*—of that position. He refers to the transhuman realm, and without that reference the attitude of faith would be void.

Again, when faith takes the shape of religions—for instance, in expressions like *misericordia,* referring to one's fellow human beings, or the German *Mitleid* (compassion, literally, sufferingwith)—the transpersonal direction takes the shape of interhuman relationships. It is not by chance that Saint Augustine contrasted Christian compassion with Stoic *ataraxia*; stressing the prompting factor—*motus*—which leads to action. It is clear that compassion is not considered a sickness of the soul. It is related to the love of God and, in this sense, transposed, as it were, from the direction toward God to the direction toward human beings in their concrete, that is, miserable, situation.

The shift from faith to religion gives one specific quality to the attitude of faith leading to acts, namely, the formulation of norms to guide acts with all the problematic aspects inherent in codes of behavior. Norms are an equivalent of rules or canon demanding obedience. Religions based on revelation find here fertile ground for the step they take from norms to commandments and, in the opposite direction, from commandments to norms. Even when we consider that shift well based, we cannot ignore the fact that any formulation makes the norm independent of the attitude, as the aspect of guidance implies. A norm gains self-sufficiency. The primary correlation between faith and acts ceases to be primary once it is related to formulated norm. The institutional character of religions makes the possible rift between the fundamental attitude and the formulation of the norm even more conspicuous. Since norms appertain not only to concrete human beings but also concrete and therefore sporadic situations, they have to apply to empirical historical situations. Therefore the application of the norm to the historical—that is, to a changing situation—becomes one of the components of concreteness that is so prominent in that context. The changing component is not confined to the practical dimension or to the process of the history of ideas. It takes the shape of the possible clash between different theories and religious traditions. The clash in the practical realm is perhaps more striking because norms by definition call for response from every human being, while the discrepancy with science may, at least at first, be confined to innovators in the scientific realm, exemplified by Copernicus and Galileo.

The relation between faith and philosophy is not essentially a clash, but it is still one of difference. Philosophy as reflection can be applied to faith and to religion, but philosophy as a synopsis of concepts may draw concepts from religions, as is the case with the concept of God or of creation. To a very large extent, the difference lies between reflection directed toward concepts, which is characteristic of philosophy, and the thematic dimension of religion, which may or may not absorb the attitude of reflection, at least in the first instance.

Nevertheless, the conclusion is a philosophical one: there are various approaches to the question of faith and religion, and no single or ultimate one. It is easier for philosophy to accept this affirmation than it is for faith, much less religion.